"I enjoyed reading the inspiring stories of these 30 Singaporeans, who shared how they came to Singapore and sunk roots in our society over time. For some, their loved ones made this journey together with them, while others married Singaporeans and set up families here. They have contributed significantly to Singapore in their respective fields and helped to make this a better place for all of us.

Singapore's racial harmony and cultural diversity are our strengths. These qualities allow us to remain cohesive while we seize new opportunities in a globalised environment by being a vibrant and innovative hub for investments, talents and ideas. We cannot achieve this goal if our society becomes inward-looking and xenophobic. More importantly, it is not who we are as a people and it does not reflect the values we stand for.

These stories of integration also reflect the experiences of many other new immigrants who have chosen to call Singapore home. Together, the narratives form part of our cultural tapestry and remind us that Singapore has been an immigrant society for centuries, and we must continue to remain open and connected with the world.

Majulah Singapura!"

—**Chee Hong Tat**
Senior Minister of State, Ministry of Transport

"*Stories of Integration* is a timely book in challenging times like these when our oneness is threatened by xenophobia and bigotry. These 30 new Singaporeans from diverse national and racial origins remind us that Singapore is a special place for all and we can be 'one united people, regardless of race, language or religion'. In choosing Singapore to be their permanent home, they bring with them the wealth of their personal history to enrich our lives with their cultural and social contributions. It behoves us to embrace them as one of our very own, sharing with them our common national space, and with it, our common humanity for the good of all."

—**William Wan, JP, PhD.**
Secretary, Singapore Kindness Movement

T0244018

"Singapore and Singaporeans have always valued the talents that immigrants bring to Singapore. I have witnessed first-hand how diligently Prakash has worked to organize bonding activities and managing welfare initiatives to help less privileged students. The book, *Stories of Integration* conceptualized by Prakash Hetamsaria and written by Vandana Aggarwal records the stories of 30 such new citizens and is a well-timed testament to their commitment to this country that they now call home. Congratulations on a great effort!"

—**Don Wee**
Member of Parliament, Chua Chu Kang GRC

"Thank you Vandana and Prakash for foregrounding these 30 inspiring and transforming stories. It brings back memories of how my forefathers first set foot on this island, their initial struggles in overcoming adversity and eventually sinking their roots here. We are an immigrant nation that has built our Singapore unique identity over a few generations. In embracing the true Singapore spirit, we continue to celebrate our cultural diversity, appreciate our differences and respect our shared values as a bedrock of a harmonious and resilient society."

—**A. J. Suhani Sujari, BBM**
Chairman, PA Residents Network Council

"Singapore has thrived economically and socially because of our collective resolve to integrate people from diverse backgrounds and make them a part of the Singapore story. In a world where xenophobia and nativism has gained traction and communities are increasingly becoming insular, the book *Stories of Integration* showcasing the stories of 30 new citizens, is a testament to how things happen differently in Singapore. This important effort by Prakash Hetamsaria and Vandana Aggarwal will add much to our knowledge of the efforts made by new migrants to adapt to our unique social and cultural fabric. It also reminds us that Singapore is ever ready to embrace those who come to our shores, willing to contribute to our nation."

—**Dr Mathew Mathews**
Principal Research Fellow & Head of Social Lab
Institute of Policy Studies

"Vandana Aggarwal's book is so timely, it's unbelievable. Countries like Singapore, Canada and the USA have been built by people coming and settling down from other places. It has been seen that over time, these very people become overly protective, and are unable to accept that newcomers. Vandana explores the contributions of the next generation of citizens and what makes them passionate about Singapore. This collection of stories show that our "new" citizens are committed, cosmopolitan and creative. In them, we discover the very same spirit of self-help and community that has always been a hallmark of Singapore."

—**Dr N. Varaprasad**
Former Chief Executive, National Library Board

"Negative stereotypes of immigrants, like percussion instruments, are oft amplified in social media. That such discourse has become more frequent is a matter of concern. In recent times, this has added to xenophobic sentiments, and aggravated racial tensions in Singapore. In this context, this compilation, which brings together the diverse journeys of 30 immigrants who have made Singapore their home, is opportune. Individually, each has made tremendous advances in their respective fields – be it medicine, healthcare, academia, business, entrepreneurship, literature or the arts. Together, they have all given so generously in their efforts to reach out to their fellow citizens. Like so many before them, their contributions have been made softly but significantly – collectively adding to the rich symphony of our nation."

—**Rajesh Rai**
Associate Professor and Head, South Asian Studies,
National University of Singapore

"Integration was the glue used by the founding fathers to transform a colonial outpost into a modern metropolis. People of all races and religions came together to form One Singapore. Astute socio-economic policies ensured all citizens a place under the Singapore sun.

I commend my friend and author Vandana and her collaborator Prakash for relating the above saga through the contributions made by thirty naturalized citizens of the nation. This book will help us look back, to look forward in these challenging times."

Council Member, Puan Noor Aishah Intercultural Institute

"People from a wide range of cultures, ethnicities, and backgrounds call Singapore home. We must cherish this diversity as a source of strength. The stories in this book help us to understand how immigrants have contributed to our society and economy, the challenges they face when settling in, and how our first-generation Singaporeans have worked hard to embrace our values and way of life. I hope readers will appreciate that Singaporeans – both 'new' and 'old' – have plenty in common, and that every one of us, regardless of our place of birth, can contribute to the next chapter of Our Singapore Story."

—Alvin Tan
Minister of State, Ministry for Culture, Community and Youth
& Ministry for Trade and Industry
Member, National Integration Council

The People's Association and its Grassroots Organisations (GROs) play a vital role in engaging and integrating new immigrants into the local community. Efforts in promoting integration in our multi-ethnic and multi-cultural community provide opportunities for locals and newcomers to forge friendships and strengthen bonds as one Singaporean, regardless of nationality. GROs also work closely with Immigrant Associations and other community partners to co-create community programmes for the benefit of residents.

The stories of integration in this book are indeed heart-warming and inspiring. Integration continues to be a collective work-in-progress, and a journey each of us can contribute and make a difference!

—Lim Hock Yu
Chief Executive Director, People's Association (PA)

Stories of
Integration

Stories of
Integration

30 SINGAPOREANS WHO MADE AN IMPACT

WRITTEN BY
VANDANA AGGARWAL

CONCEPT BY
PRAKASH K HETAMSARIA

Published in 2022 by Marshall Cavendish Editions
An imprint of Marshall Cavendish International

A member of the
Times Publishing Group

National Library Board, Singapore Cataloguing-in-Publication Data

Name(s): Aggarwal, Vandana, 1962- | Hetamsaria, Prakash Kumar.
Title: Stories of integration : 30 Singaporeans who made an impact / written by
Vandana Aggarwal ; concept by Prakash K Hetamsaria.
Description: Singapore : Marshall Cavendish Editions, 2022.
Identifier(s): ISBN 978-981-4974-61-5 (paperback)
Subject(s): LCSH: Singaporeans—Anecdotes. | Immigrants—Singapore—
Anecdotes. | Singapore—Anecdotes.
Classification: DDC 959.5705—dc23

Printed in Singapore

CONTENTS

Foreword   13

Preface   15

A doctor for all seasons
Associate Professor Zubair Amin   **19**

Betting big on Singapore
Victor Mills   **25**

Breaking barriers, building bridges
Sazzad Hossain   **31**

The more you dream, the farther you get
Dr Le Thi Nguyet Minh   **37**

We are like this only
Daisy Irani Subaiah & Subin Subaiah   **43**

A global sensation, made in Singapore
Pranoti Nagarkar   **49**

Integrating through community bonding
Dr Sun Guang Wen   **55**

Mirroring Singapore's soul through stories
Kamaladevi Aravindan   **62**

Creating a nation by design
Larry Yeung   **68**

Robotics and the Smart Nation
Dr Marcelo H Ang Jr   **74**

Forging a musical pathway to integration
Dr Robert Casteels   **80**

A heart and soul that beats for Singapore
Jaspreet Chhabra, PBM 86

Creating connections between Singaporeans
and nature
Gan Cheong Weei 92

It started with raincoats!
Dipa Swaminathan 98

Cross-cultural interactions through art
Milenko Prvacki 104

Shaping the future of banking
Amit Sinha 110

Making the impossible possible
Khoo Swee Chiow 116

Contributing to the Singapore story
Dr Bhanu Ranjan 122

Service with a smile
Chew Ai Mei 128

The art, the artist, and his vision
Rosihan Dahim 133

Nurturing our youth through sports
Aleksandar Duric 139

Learn, adapt and practise: The mantra for success
Cornelio Gutierrez Padre 145

The langoli *lao shi*
Vijayalakshmi Mohan 151

Embracing the core Singapore value
of cohesiveness
Tony Du Zhiqiang 157

A family rooted by a sense of belonging
and ownership
Veena Prakash 162

Dancing in step with time
Aravinth Kumarasamy 168

Service, leadership and giving back
to the community
Sameen Khan, PBM 175

Giving till it hurts
Rajan Jain 181

Creating a kinder society
Cesar Balota 186

Eyeing better medical care for all
Dr Rupesh Agrawal 192

About the team 198

FOREWORD

Mr S Rajaratnam, one of Singapore's Founding Fathers, once said: "being Singaporean is a matter not of ancestry, but of choice and conviction." It remains apt and poignant today, and perhaps more so, in an age when identity and belonging are contested concepts.

It is therefore timely that journey of thirty of our naturalised citizens are captured in *Stories of Integration*. Every Singaporean, whether local-born or naturalised, has a role to play in making our city-state our best possible home.

I congratulate Mr Prakash Hetamsaria for conceptualising the idea, and Mrs Vandana Aggarwal for her efforts in crafting these inspiring stories through extensive research and interviews with each person.

I am confident this will help newcomers to Singapore, as reading about the experience of their predecessors will help them understand how they too can fulfil their responsibilities and add value to our multicultural and multiracial society. I am also certain that this book will be interesting to Singaporeans whose families have been here for generations, in showing how, even as the fabric of Singapore society evolves and changes, fundamental values remain our shared heritage.

Ms Sim Ann
Senior Minister of State, Ministry of Foreign Affairs and
Ministry of National Development

PREFACE

Singapore, as we see it today, is a grand success story. It is intriguing how a young island nation with few natural resources and a small population has not just stayed alive but thrived in an increasingly competitive world. There is no doubt that it is blessed with visionary leaders, under whose watchful eyes the country has remained agile, relevant and robust.

To stay relevant and move ahead, Singapore needs a highly skilled and educated workforce. In today's world, no nation can survive without innovation, enterprise and growth. As borders shrink and the world becomes increasingly connected, Singapore has shown how overseas talent can be harnessed for mutual benefit.

Singapore has maintained a policy of complementing the local workforce with overseas talent to compete against the larger and more resourceful nations. Foreigners who come to work here are attracted to the peaceful, disciplined and multi-ethnic vibe, and often end up planting their roots in this island nation. It becomes a win-win situation as they bring with them, expertise in their chosen field of work, replenish the falling population numbers and boost the economy.

I was enthused when Prakash Hetamsaria, himself a naturalized citizen and active community volunteer, first mooted the idea of a book featuring talented, naturalized Singaporeans. I have known Prakash for over a decade, and he has always genuinely and with single-minded devotion, worked towards the integration of newcomers with local-born Singaporeans. For me, it was the perfect opportunity to showcase the efforts and stories of people who have left their birth countries and set down roots in a foreign land.

We consciously chose people across nationalities, religions and work expertise, and endeavoured to bring forth the different flavours that they have brought to Singapore. Over lengthy interviews, the final thirty bared their hearts on their reasons for emigrating, their determination to deepen their roots in their new home, and their efforts at proactively engaging and integrating with the locals.

As I wrote chapter after chapter, it became clear that these Singaporeans contribute not just their expertise and experience, they also bring with them diverse cultural traditions and value systems that enhance and enrich Singapore society manifold. With an abiding sense of pride, they put their clenched fists to their heart and take the oath of allegiance to Singapore while contributing meaningfully to its development and growth.

I am grateful to Baldeo Prasad for making numerous trips across the island to capture the interviewees though his lens. My gratitude to everyone who supported us, recommended individuals, put us in touch with them and helped us in countless other ways. Last but not the least, to all the people I interviewed, you inspire me, and I have learnt life lessons from each one of you. Keep doing what you do!

This book is a tribute to all immigrants who have come to Singapore with hopes in their hearts, a will to adapt, and a willingness to work hand in hand with fellow Singaporeans to take this nation to greater heights and make its lofty aspirations real.

Vandana Aggarwal
Author

A DOCTOR FOR ALL SEASONS

"From my father, I learnt to live by the principle of leaving any place I visit in a better condition than I found it. I live by that tenet in all aspects of my personal and professional life."

**Assoc Professor
Zubair Amin**

During the fasting month of Ramadan in 2020, Associate Professor Zubair Amin was hard at work putting in long days at his office. On weekends, he would volunteer at migrant worker dormitories seeing patients affected by Covid-19. Dr Zubair, who heads the Department of Neonatology at the National University Hospital (NUH) in Singapore, also teaches pediatrics at the Yong Loo Lin School of Medicine and packs in a very busy day.

It was a war-like situation, he recalls. With no prior experience of handling the virus, doctors and nurses had to be at the forefront and figure out the best way to cope. An unexpected spike in infections at the migrant worker dormitories led to a desperate call for medical staff and volunteers who could communicate with workers, of whom many were from Zubair's native country Bangladesh. He realized that along with his medical skills, his proficiency in his mother tongue Bangla would come in handy. Zubair rolled up his sleeves and underwent training to conduct swab tests, volunteering up to 14 hours on weekends and treating hundreds of migrant workers.

Where there is a will there is a way

Not one to sit still, Zubair soon realized that there was an incredible need to see patients quickly, assess them, and provide medication and advice. From looking after preemies, he was now taking care of adults. He, along with the other medical staff, struggled to find his feet in an unprecedented situation. "We learnt to learn from each other. There was no hierarchy as we were all on flat ground keeping our instruments and workplace clean, dispensing medications and talking to patients. The patients were not just from Bangladesh but many countries like India and China as well. It was an incremental learning journey," recalls Zubair.

On a whim, he wrote an e-mail to doctors and nurses requesting them to keep certain things in mind while taking care of Muslim patients during Ramadan. In no time that e-mail went viral, drawing attention to the need for understanding the practices of other races and cultures. He was also closely involved in the BAI initiative at NUH, which stands for Befrienders and Ambassadors for Inpatients; coincidentally, *bai* is Bangla for 'brother'. It consists of an eclectic group of doctors and nurses from various disciplines who speak to the migrant patients in their mother tongue so as to keep their spirits up as they fight the virus. This brotherhood helped the patients feel connected as they shared their woes in a language they were comfortable in, explains Zubair, who believes that by serving others he benefits in numerous ways.

Once his engagement in the dorms became public, there were concerns that he could potentially bring back the virus to his regular clinic and compromise the safety of his tiny patients. He needn't have worried. Zubair was overwhelmed by the support and words of encouragement he received from the parents of his little wards.

Planting seeds for the future

Born in Mymensingh, a well-known education hub in Bangladesh, Zubair was deeply influenced by the calmness of his rich natural surroundings and stories of women empowerment. His early years had a lasting influence on him as he grew up with kids from varied backgrounds. Life was relaxed and the community was close-knit where everyone looked out for everyone. This laid the seeds for his natural instinct to step up and help when required.

Even as a child he had a deep urge to do something meaningful and medicine seemed to be a natural choice. This is what first brought him to Singapore in 1992. Singapore was a centre for an entrance examination to further his education in the United States. Even though he did not visit any hospitals during his two-month sojourn here, he happened to meet some compatriot migrant workers. Those first impressions of their lives were to later become a catalyst for bigger things to come.

As luck would have it, he gained admission to an International Educational Partnership in Pediatrics (IEPP) programme at the University of Illinois at Chicago — a unique programme combining pediatrics and a degree in health professions education. It was a wonderful learning experience and his years in America matured him, says Zubair.

His short exposure to Singapore had shown him a side of this island that attracted him and Singapore beckoned. Aware that Asia was on the cusp of making its presence felt and conscious that Singapore was well-known for striving for excellence in every field, the can-do mentality and efficient system all attracted the idealistic Zubair. He felt he was much more needed in this part of the world where he wouldn't be one among many but could contribute much more. Armed with his newly acquired professional degrees, Zubair, who was by then married with a child, joined the KK Women's and Children's Hospital in Singapore.

Reflecting on his decision, the academic thinks it was the best investment he has made. At that time in Asia, the discipline of medical pedagogy was almost non-existent and Zubair was one of the few doctors who was professionally qualified to both teach as well as develop a curriculum and assessment. Very quickly, he got involved with the nascent Medical Education Unit at the School of Medicine at the National University of Singapore (NUS), later rising to the position of Assistant Dean for Curriculum and Assessment at the School of Medicine, where he involved himself in the fine-tuning of the medical curriculum, assessment methodologies and training of doctors.

Foreseeing the altering demographics of the Singapore population, Zubair was a member of the team which created a unique interdisciplinary module for geriatric care in Year 2 of the undergraduate medical curriculum. He is proud that he was party to the vision that anticipated the ageing population and planned for it. Zubair is also involved with medical schools and professional bodies in other countries, using his talent and experience to guide and mentor them in the development of their own curriculum and assessment methodologies.

Now a father to three children, two girls and a boy, Zubair feels blessed that he has had the opportunity to love two countries and benefit from them in equal measure. He treasures his growing up years in Bangladesh where he learnt to see the world through the lens of similarity, instead of differences. Zubair makes a conscious effort to educate Singaporeans, that it's not just the migrant workers from Bangladesh but well-educated people like him who also contribute to Singapore.

"In all my years in Singapore I have not encountered any discrimination, only love, respect and support. I have developed cherished relationships with colleagues, patients, students, neighbours and many others. It's the people who prompted me to take up citizenship," says Zubair who became a citizen in the year 2000.

He recounts how as a young doctor he would eat at Ananda Bhavan, a popular restaurant in Little India. Even today, years later, whenever he visits, the chef steps out to talk to him and enquires about his welfare. The standing joke in his family is that they cannot go out anywhere without Zubair being approached by someone who has known him, whether as a friend, teacher or doctor. It is this human touch that he loves.

Along with his interest in philately, he is passionate about nature and sustainability. In his small way he tries to be environmentally conscious and bikes around the island for exercise, often finding himself clearing up beaches, park connector networks and pathways. These outings double up as opportunities to explore the many natural surroundings and he brings his children along when he can.

Zubair's family has integrated well in Singapore. His wife is a post-doctoral researcher at NUS. His two older daughters study Mandarin as their second language. His son, who is in primary school, takes Higher Chinese as his mother tongue. They are deeply rooted in Singapore's ethos and he is sure that they, like him, will contribute meaningfully here when the time comes.

"The Covid-19 pandemic is a lesson that good times do not last forever. The carnival is over. Employers and employees will hopefully have a better sense of reality. There is nothing like a bit of hardship to make Singaporeans look again at what they have. This crisis will help to reinvent society and the economy."

Victor Mills

BETTING BIG ON SINGAPORE

"Singapore is not the norm, it is the exception," insists Victor Mills, referring to Singapore's multicultural, egalitarian and meritocratic society. The Northern Ireland-born Singapore citizen neither minces words when praising Singapore nor when drawing attention to what he perceives are drawbacks that could pull it down. Either way his passion for Singapore is obvious.

He counts his journey to becoming a Singaporean his biggest achievement. When he first arrived, he never thought that it would be for the long haul. It was a journey that took 20 years and was by no means a hurried decision taken for the sake of convenience. Victor has a major problem with being referred to as a new citizen. "Who is a new citizen? Everyone pays taxes, follows the law and integrates into society. Is there a cut-off date for being a new citizen after which you become old?" questions the man who took up Singapore citizenship in 2012.

Reposing confidence in Singapore's economy

Victor is the CEO of Singapore International Chamber of Commerce (SICC) which connects businesses with one another, helping them grow by providing opportunities to learn and share expertise. SICC promotes collaboration among large companies and local small and medium enterprises as they are the backbone of any country and they employ the most people. He strongly believes partnerships are vitally important for mutual benefit.

While the world economy faces significant challenges in light of the Covid-19 crisis, Victor is understandably most concerned for Singapore because of its export-oriented, open economy — and, given its small size, its vulnerability. The fact that the government has stepped in to help is a measure of how serious the problem is, he explains. Victor counts Singapore among the lucky countries which have the financial muscle to handle the crisis. "Living within its means and having thrifty leaders has benefitted Singapore in the long run. But there are existential challenges, and we must gear up for a more competitive world and stand up against the economic superpowers such as China and the US," he cautions.

Victor serves on the Board of Trustees of the ISEAS-Yusof Ishak Institute, is a member of the Advisory Board for the Singapore Management University Academy and a director at the ESSEC Business School. He is also a member of the Singapore Institute of Directors and the Singapore Institute of International Affairs.

Taking the positives from the pandemic

Not all economic matters concern Victor. While people lament the troubles brought about by the pandemic, Victor prefers to look at the brighter side of things. "It's a great time for leadership to step up and show how active citizenry can be achieved without chaos. The government has done all the heavy lifting over the last 55 years. Economic growth has created an exceptionally well-endowed Singapore. We should craft a unique path for the next 50 years."

He attributes the right attitude and approach to the Singapore government but is pragmatic enough to warn that the successes of the past cannot be sustained without adjustments and sacrifices. "It is 1965, all over again," he says, referring to the year when Singapore was faced with an unexpected separation from Malaysia. "We have no choice but to make it work. As in a marriage, we must keep working on it continuously," reminds Victor.

He strongly believes that the pandemic is a wake-up call. According to him, it was complacency that was holding back the development of business and a greater understanding of the outside world. There was a misplaced sense of entitlement — a by-product of becoming so successful so quickly. Victor hopes Singaporeans will take a step back and be prepared to do their bit and not expect the government to do all the thinking for them.

Another silver lining that has come out of the pandemic, he feels, is that it has brought migrant foreign workers into the limelight. The pandemic is a great leveller as it has affected everyone. "By getting an inside view of the workers' dormitories we have become a more compassionate society. We did not know people lived like that. The Singapore government with its extraordinary ability to pivot has taken strong and quick steps to resolve the situation. This is the strength of Singapore which has helped it in the past and will continue to propel it further in the foreseeable future," he says.

The great Singapore mosaic

Since Singapore became home, Victor has bent backwards to integrate. He was lucky to have met his future wife three days after arriving here and married her within a year. The tropical heat, which he took years to get used to, was made more tolerable by the warm welcome of his newfound family. His wife, who is third-generation Singaporean from the Hainanese community, tactfully and gradually increased the level of spiciness in his food and he confesses that now his capacity for spicy food is greater than hers. Thanks to his wife and her family, Victor remains deeply assimilated in the local culture and can understand and speak a smattering of Mandarin.

The Northern Irish are known for being occasionally stubborn and blunt. When not helping businesses grow and sustain in Singapore, Victor can be relied upon to share his opinions on Singapore in an honest and direct way. He feels it's important to have a view and to articulate it. "I judge people with what they say and do, and not as Indians, Chinese or Malays. I see the human before anything else. Instead of focusing so much on our differences we should focus on our similarities as human beings and our shared, universal human values. If we do this and keep the channels of communication open, we can prevent a polarized society and create a more inclusive one."

For him, communication is all about effectiveness. His Singlish is reasonably good and he uses it when required, especially in hawker centres, referring to these communal places as "the great connectors for it is here that all Singaporeans regardless of age, race, language, religion or economic status sit side by side and eat. We should cherish our multicultural and multi-ethnic society and revel in it," says Victor.

When he moved to Singapore from Hong Kong in 1985, he was impressed by the equal opportunities available to all, and the friendly and open social structure.

Any anti-foreigner sentiment bothers Victor. He finds it a real threat to the peace and sustainability of Singapore. Having grown up in Northern Ireland, torn apart by political violence during his youth, Victor has the advantage of having seen the other side of the coin at close quarters. Although the experience has made him wary of organized religion, it has opened his mind to accepting people from a different community to his.

And that's why he says it is imperative Singaporeans don't give up the values of openness and multiculturalism, as those are the values that have helped build Singapore and will sustain it in the future. "Not many countries have good race relations and since Singapore has nurtured these so well, it would be foolish to weaken them," says Victor. He strongly believes that it is important for Singaporeans to live and work overseas to develop points of comparison to be able to appreciate what they have in Singapore.

He acknowledges that you need two hands to clap, and that there are some expatriates who live in a bubble, give themselves a bad name, and reinforce negative perceptions and stereotypes. "New immigrants must invest and contribute their skills for the benefit of the community depending on their skills and capabilities. We live because of the hard work and thrift of the Pioneer and Merdeka generations and we cannot take our country for granted," says Victor candidly.

He was a part of the Singapore Citizen Journey, a working group created to revamp the journey all naturalized citizens must take to truly associate with being Singaporean. "We cannot allow new citizens to live in cocoons. As foreigners trying to make this our home, we have to keep building bridges. We should craft a unique path and be prepared to do our bit."

BREAKING BARRIERS, BUILDING BRIDGES

"Volunteering gives people exposure to direct beneficiaries, helps them to see the situation on the ground, develops empathy and compassion, and helps society develop a soul."

Sazzad Hossain

Sazzad Hossain had always dreamt of being a doctor and making a difference in people's lives. Though he ultimately decided not to pursue that professional track, he is still impacting and improving lives through his chosen path. The smart and suave young man of Bangladeshi origin is a far cry from the 11-year-old who came to Singapore in 2005 and had difficulty speaking English.

His own struggles with a new language motivated Sazzad to embark on a journey of working with migrant workers to help bridge the communication gap and create a more inclusive society.

Sazzad calls himself a "social entrepreneur, author, dreamer and visionary". He is focused on teaching migrant workers English communication skills which he hopes will make for a safer workplace, foster better understanding between workers and Singaporeans and, in the long run, help workers become computer literate and develop entrepreneurship skills for self-sufficiency.

Empowering through enabling

Sazzad first came in contact with the Bangladeshi workers who congregated in his neighbourhood of Lakeside on their days off to relax, play cricket and socialize.

"When I came to Singapore, I had the privilege of being with family. Yet, I was struggling. I had left my friends and all that was familiar behind and was trying to adapt to a whole new situation. Imagine the predicament of the workers who are stuck in a foreign land with no support base. Not only is it psychologically taxing, but it also creates difficulties in the workplace. They are unable to follow safety instructions or understand the terms of their contracts leading to exploitation. When I heard the stories of the workers it resonated. I did not want to just be a bystander," he explains.

The sensitive teenager was particularly moved by the plight of workers from Bangladesh because they were totally isolated from the locals, unlike the Chinese or Tamil workers who could at least make themselves understood in Singapore. Sazzad started teaching English informally to six of them during the weekends. As word got around and more workers joined the sessions, Sazzad realized that if he wanted to make a difference, he had to offer something more structured.

He took upon himself the task of making worksheets to teach functional, everyday English language skills, and spent hours writing a simple guide for the workers to read in their free time.

In 2013, while still a student at St Andrew's Junior College, Sazzad launched the Social Development Initiative Academy, a social enterprise where he serves as CEO today. The Academy is making its presence felt in four countries having trained over 8,500 students and improving the lives of thousands of migrant workers. Yet, Sazzad sees it as only a drop in the ocean. About 2,000 students graduate per year from the SDI Academy and Sazzad hopes to increase this by a few multiples through more learning centres and satellite learning corners set up in dormitories. His classes are currently run by volunteers and part-time teachers.

His journey wasn't without struggle. In the process of setting up SDI Academy, his grades in school suffered, and his parents, although liberal and supportive, felt that he should focus on his studies. Furthermore, he had no funds and no teaching experience. Despite this, he was not willing to give up.

He focused on his studies and secured a place at the Nanyang Technological University (NTU) where he is currently studying for a degree in Electrical Engineering. He is thankful to NTU for supporting his initiative by providing, without charge, space where he could conduct classes.

Once the young lad got noticed for his work, accolades followed. SDI Academy won the "Most Socially Responsible

Start-up" award in 2014, and in 2015 won a grant of $50,000 at the DBS-NUS Social Venture Challenge Asia.

Sazzad is also CEO of Linger.ai, a B2B language software and classroom management company which he founded in 2018. It is a platform for language learning which can be localized to meet specific language needs. The goal is to create a hybrid learning system supported by technology that can reach out to groups all over the world.

In addition, he is one of the youngest fellows of the Royal Society for the Encouragement of Arts, Manufactures and Commerce and a fellow of the Kairos Society Global Class of 2019, which is a global community comprising of the students and global leaders desiring to solve the major challenges faced by the world.

Sazzad, who took up Singapore citizenship in 2007, was the youngest Singaporean to be awarded the Ashoka Fellowship in 2018, a lifelong, prestigious international programme that connects him with the world's leading social entrepreneurs and has given him a wide support network and credibility.

He is also one of 200 leaders selected from 33 Asia-Pacific countries as part of the inaugural cohort of the Obama Foundation in 2019. The year-long programme, among other things, connected, guided, supported and empowered emerging leaders like Sazzad who have the potential to change the world.

He has been chosen to be an honoree in the Forbes' 30 Under 30 Asia List, 2021, which is made up of young leaders who have persevered and thrived despite the uncertainty of the Covid-19 pandemic.

Focusing on the bigger picture

Sazzad is a man brimming with ideas. He wants to make a larger impact for the migrant workers, starting from the time they set foot in Singapore, when they need much support to equipping them with useful entrepreneurship skills, when they return to their home countries.

SDI Academy is working with the Ministry of Manpower (MOM) and Migrant Worker's Centre to create an integration programme to train newcomers on safety regulations and social norms. In a step forward, they have been given access to worker dormitories and allowed to advertise their courses in MOM newsletters. Additionally, they hold roadshows on safety issues to equip migrant workers with the necessary skills and understanding to do their work confidently.

As Sazzad explains, "What we are doing is not rocket science. We are working on social inclusion which should be a norm. We want negative perceptions about workers to change and for more Singaporeans to be aware that diversity enriches our society."

There are plans to conduct workshops at schools and institutes of higher learning to create awareness in the younger generation of the need to integrate workers in our society and inspire them to start their own initiatives to help the workers.

SDI Academy has partnered with institutes of higher learning such as the PSB Academy where 56 migrant workers have been furthering their studies on a part-time basis to attain professional diplomas. One of the students was invited to speak at a TEDxNUS event in 2017. They are now paying forward and helping their fellow workers carve out a future career path for themselves in their home countries.

"We are giving them entrepreneurship skills and may in the future become a platform of skilled workers for countries like India, Bangladesh and Indonesia to tap into," elaborates Sazzad. There are expansion plans on the horizon. He dreams of a day when he can set up learning centres in worker dormitories with access to free space so that workers can practise speaking English on their own. Plans are in the pipeline to acquire space for a learning centre in the Farrer Park area.

Unfortunately, just when everything seemed to be going as planned, Covid-19 happened and threw a spanner in the works. The migrant workers were amongst the worst affected. As face-to-face classes were temporarily discontinued, Sazzad and his team turned their attention to more immediate needs. He estimates that in the first eight months since Covid struck in early 2020, they distributed over 45,000 food packets and over 10,000 hygiene kits and masks to the workers.

"Singapore has progressed enormously over the last 50 years. How we treat our migrant workers is a reflection of how our society is evolving. They work hard to build Singapore. We need to humanize migrant workers, be caring about their future and work together to build their future," opines Sazzad.

The silver lining to the pandemic was that it unexpectedly shone the spotlight on the plight of migrant workers. Seeing how they could not go out of the dormitory to purchase groceries or food catered to their taste, Sazzad launched a new mobile app called DoorMart. It offered affordable grocery delivery and nutritious food options to workers.

"We at SDI want to leave the planet a better place than we found it and inspire people to work towards this goal too. We need to pay our dues. Singapore was built on the hard labour of many people and we must continue building on it and give it a soul. For that, it is important to have a heart to care for all people regardless of race or religion," says Sazzad passionately.

This trailblazing young social entrepreneur is a positive role model for our younger generation and is leading the way to cultivate a kinder, more caring and giving society.

THE MORE YOU DREAM, THE FARTHER YOU GET

"I think I am different from many others. I live a full life, contribute to society, and making others happy gives me happiness. I don't just chase dreams, I achieve them."

Dr Le Thi Nguyet Minh

As the top biology student in Vietnam, Dr Le Thi Nguyet Minh took a study loan to pursue her dreams and a degree in Life Sciences in Singapore. The homesick, nervous teenager who initially struggled with English is now an Assistant Professor at the National University of Singapore (NUS).

Minh's research group has developed a new technology using red cell extracellular vesicles as vehicles for gene therapy. She is the leading researcher in extracellular vesicle research and advisor at Carmine Therapeutics, a company she co-founded. Carmine Therapeutics was registered in Singapore in 2019 and recognized among the 15 most promising biotech companies globally in 2020. It has signed a $1.2 billion business deal to develop and eventually commercialize treatment for rare genetic diseases. This is a cause very dear to Minh's heart, as her mother suffers from a rare motor-neuron disease.

A researcher in the making

Minh believes the study of genomes will be the way forward in providing a cure for many diseases in the future. She would like to work with other groups to create a strong platform for furthering gene therapy research.

"Genomic studies in the last 20 years have uncovered lots of new genes that we can use to target a disease, recover the good genes and suppress bad ones," elaborates Minh. While it is still early days and more research and investment are required before human trials are conducted, she is optimistic that her work will go a long way in helping her mother and others suffering from degenerative diseases.

"Singapore has a great infrastructure and talent pool. I think we can put Singapore on the world map of groundbreaking work in gene therapy," says Minh.

Struggles and successes

Minh's parents served in the Vietnam army and healthcare system, and placed a lot of emphasis on education. From them, she learnt the virtues of perseverance, leadership, management and organization. After completing her high school in Hanoi, she moved to Singapore in 2001 to further her studies at NUS.

Coming to Singapore, recalls Minh, was a life changer. That was a time when the Singapore government's focus was on investing in Life Sciences. In Vietnam, most of her education had been theoretical. She now had access to a laboratory and world-class equipment. Minh loved the magnificent infrastructure and facilities afforded by NUS. Soon, the dictionary became her best friend and the lab her second home where she would study Molecular Biology and test out what she learnt through various experiments. She was given an opportunity to present a paper at a prestigious scientific conference, a rare honour for an undergraduate to compete with researchers much senior to her. She nevertheless won the best poster award, got noticed and earned herself a scholarship from the Lee Foundation.

Even then, it was not enough to make ends meet. Minh, who was still struggling with the English language, found herself taking up jobs that required her to clean toilets and wash dishes. Her then-boyfriend and now husband, a research scholar from China, was her biggest support and helped her both emotionally and financially. Those years of struggle taught Minh a lot about the value of money, the dignity of labour, and made her determined to succeed.

After graduating from NUS, Minh was fortunate to receive the Singapore-MIT Alliance scholarship and pursued a PhD at the A*STAR Genome Institute of Singapore. "The facilities at A*STAR were on par with Massachusetts Institute of Technology

(MIT) and Harvard. I had the passion for research and the ability to ask questions. I was lucky to work with a talented pool of individuals," says Minh. The cumulative result of her hard work was the new discovery of microRNA functions with important implications in neurobiology and cancer research.

In 2009, Minh and her husband became Singapore citizens. In that same year, she was one of three winners of the inaugural L'Oréal Singapore For Women In Science National Fellowship. It was an award for young female researchers who were outstanding in their chosen field and showed the potential to excel in and contribute to scientific studies in Singapore.

While pursuing her PhD, Minh was given a chance to travel to the US to conduct research at MIT and found a postdoctoral position at Harvard Medical School.

Life in the US was not easy. By then a young mother, Minh remembers that to make ends meet she would buy clearance groceries and pick up furniture and clothes from thrift stores. Her mother's failing health also meant that as the filial, older child, she felt duty-bound to finance her parents and travel home to Vietnam frequently.

She put in long hours in the lab, juggling them with childcare and housework. But looking at the positive side, Minh feels that the highly competitive atmosphere in the US taught her to handle pressure and helped her make lifelong friends. With its rich concentration of talent and enriching work environment, she could imbibe part of that work culture and bring it back to Singapore.

Her interest in education made her want to give back to her birth country. Having seen first-hand how difficult it was to obtain academic materials, Minh decided to get good quality books translated into Vietnamese. With the support of Professor

Harvey Lodish, whom she had met at MIT, she raised funds, and with a group of volunteer translators, organized a translation of his seminal book *Molecular Cell Biology* into Vietnamese. The project, which has been ongoing for over ten years, has made available the latest and most advanced information in biology to science students in Vietnam.

From 2015 to 2019, Minh worked as an Assistant Professor at the Department of Biomedical Sciences at City University of Hong Kong where she had an opportunity to set up her own lab and invent a new drug delivery platform in collaboration with her husband.

Singapore calling

Minh is blessed to have a husband who is a researcher himself and incredibly supportive of her. "We had already applied for and acquired our first Housing Development Board flat here. It is our only home in the whole wide world, bought out of our own money, and we are grateful to the Singapore government for making reasonably priced homes available to its citizens," explains Minh. Moreover, Singapore is culturally very Asian, and this resonated deeply with the couple who decided to make Singapore their home in 2009.

Having worked overseas and gained a lot of exposure and experience, she felt that Singapore brought out the best in her. Comparing Singapore to other parts of the world, she says, "Singapore practises what it preaches, does not discriminate between locals and foreigners, encourages research and gives a lot of freedom to pursue your creativity."

She is appreciative of the quality of students, the dedication of staff, and government policies, which allow scientists to work both independently and in collaboration with industry. The tremendous support she received from NUS has allowed Minh to work with the excellent local scientist community to conduct her research and partner with Singaporean entrepreneurs to build Carmine Therapeutics.

Minh has an open mind which helps her create a balance between her Vietnamese culture, her husband's Chinese roots and their life in Singapore. "Every culture is a treasure. There are conflicts but I always try to look at the positive side of things. I can understand some Mandarin though I don't speak it fluently," she says. Her children, a son and a daughter aged 4 and 11 respectively, take Mandarin as their second language and help her practise her language skills.

Her biggest concern is for her kids to not take for granted the comforts that Singapore has to offer. She tries to inculcate in them a sense of pride in Singapore and gratitude for what it has given them.

Minh is a lady with a purpose, one who is determined to give back as much, if not more, than she has received from her adopted country.

WE
ARE
LIKE
THIS
ONLY

"Integration is like yoga — it does not take effect overnight. You have to build it up slowly so that the mind and body accept it and the heart and the soul are touched."

Daisy Irani Subaiah

"Humour, particularly satire, has proven to be the best way to reflect on the flaws and foibles of ourselves and the society we live in. By laughing at ourselves we see more easily the ridiculousness of our decisions."

Subin Subaiah

Being Mrs Gandhi, a play about Mahatma Gandhi through the eyes of his wife Kasturba, is set against the backdrop of India's freedom struggle. Among other things, it brings out the need for non-violence, reasoning and tolerance as a means of conflict resolution. Staged in Singapore in 2019, it was written and directed by Subin Subaiah. The title role was portrayed by his actress wife, Daisy Irani Subaiah. The couple agrees that in multiracial Singapore, one can never emphasize these Gandhian values enough.

Like every Singaporean, they are keen to maintain Singapore's multiracial harmony. They hope that Singapore as a country can continue to harness the best minds to ensure it remains on top of its game even in the future.

Subin's job brought the couple to Singapore, from India, in 1990. It is where they have lived ever since and raised their two children, a son and a daughter. "Life in Singapore had a wonderful feel to it, and I was afraid that I would get too comfortable to move which would set me back from a career perspective," says Subin. However, his mother and wife fell in love with Singapore. "Every proposed move was vetoed until I fell in line," he adds.

Living under one roof with Singaporeans

Looking back Daisy says, "In a new country, you are put in a situation where you are out of your comfort zone and so you need a dream to keep going." Already an established stage actress in India, Daisy once again found herself starting from scratch. While on a Dependent's Pass, there were very few avenues open to her. And not one to sit twiddling her thumbs, she started volunteering at a school for differently-abled children at Toa Payoh. It was her first interaction with the locals and an eye-opener.

"To integrate I would pepper my talk with *lah* and *leh* until someone pointed out that my intonation and contexts were all wrong. I realized that I was trying too hard. Integration has to be an organic process coming from the heart." Daisy, who has embraced Singapore like a long-lost daughter, breaks into Singlish at the drop of a hat.

Simultaneously, Daisy tapped her contacts in Mumbai and started bringing Gujarati plays to Singapore. The Gujarati community, that has called Singapore home for generations, lapped it up and she performed to sell-out shows. When Singapore's first sitcom *Under One Roof* was offered to her, it was the perfect break the actress needed to showcase her talent to a wider audience.

It was during the filming of *Under One Roof* and its ensuing success, that Daisy finally understood how essential racial harmony was to Singapore. The whole concept of a Chinese, Malay and Indian family living and interacting socially made her conscious of the social reality and need for healthy integration. Her vibrant personality and open mind helped her to not only soak in the local culture but appreciate it. "It was all about allowing my heart to welcome in people," she says.

Seeing her potential, the then Television Corporation of Singapore offered her a full-time job. Daisy was soon the Executive Producer for several highly rated TV programmes. The many comedy, drama and documentary series she produced and directed garnered many prestigious awards.

She was also chosen to launch Okto, a channel for children and art lovers, and redefine Vasantham to position it as a full-day channel with new and interesting content. It was a challenging and exciting phase in her career as she was involved with every aspect of creating the new channels, which were launched in October 2008 to rave reviews.

Meanwhile, Subin was busy with his professional commitments. Singapore had started to grow on him too. "I felt right at home in Singapore's multiracial society. It had a leadership which had a tight grip on managing the country's future and an arts space that was fast becoming vibrant. A bonus was the media industry that was ready to leverage my wife's talents, and the best food you can expect to find anywhere in the world," explains Subin.

The list could go on and on. In short, it wasn't a hard decision for the couple to drop anchor and re-orient themselves into becoming Singaporeans in 2004.

Tackling sensitive issues with humour

To create content relevant to Singapore and convey messages with humour, the couple launched HuM Theatre in 2009. Subin adapted as well as wrote original material for the stage, all laced with his trademark wit, to shine a light on the peculiarities in society. Over the years, the couple has consciously chosen to create content that resonates with Singaporeans.

Noticing the emerging fault lines between local Indian Singaporeans and the new Indian immigrants, they directed — and acted — in the play *We Are Like This Only!*. Staged in 2013 in forum theatre fashion, the idea was to bring issues into the open and generate post-show discussions. It helped that the couple was in a unique position of being able to view the topic of immigration and integration as Singaporeans as well as foreigners.

They went on to make a sequel in 2016, this time written entirely by Subin. "When the community and the country believe in you and allow you to put forward the naked truth for all to see, you have a duty towards them," explains Subin. "If immigration is important to our country, then integration becomes of even more vital importance. We wanted to establish that integration within the Indian community was a two-way street, and with the right attitude could be a reality sooner rather than later."

Addressing points of friction in a comedic way seemed to be the best way to assist the process. *We Are Like This Only 2* accomplished that purpose, and it was honoured by the National Integration Council. Indeed, all programmes put up by HuM Theatre have established its credibility as one of Singapore's own homegrown theatre companies.

Along with her professional life, Daisy has never forgotten to support the underprivileged members of society. She loves volunteering at the Lorong Melayu Neighbourhood Committee and is the Community Director for Chinese New Year and Christmas parties. When she visits old-age homes, elderly residents still recognize her as Daisy from *Under One Roof.* She is also active with the local chapter of the Rotary Club, volunteering her time for sundry events which she enjoys. "When I volunteer, I see the different faces of Singapore — different professions, education and financial levels. It opens my eyes to what I have and how much I could give back to society," says Daisy.

Their children are grown up and busy in their respective professions; yet between family, work, volunteering and social commitments, there is always something that needs their attention. The unexpected Covid-19 crisis meant that their latest HuM Theatre production had to be shelved. Making the most of the situation, they took the opportunity to focus on the 3 R's — Rest, Review and Rejuvenate. It was a time to meditate, do yoga, lounge with the family and generally just let go of *barang barang* (things) in their lives while planning how to continue organizing theatre in changing times.

Daisy confesses to having wondered in the past about what makes her a Singaporean, and if she will ever be accepted as one. She has pondered on the question of how many years of living and serving the nation is required for one to be truly Singaporean. Finding no real answers, Daisy and Subin focus on doing what they do best — creating channels for introspection, and debate laced with a great degree of humour.

A GLOBAL SENSATION, MADE IN SINGAPORE

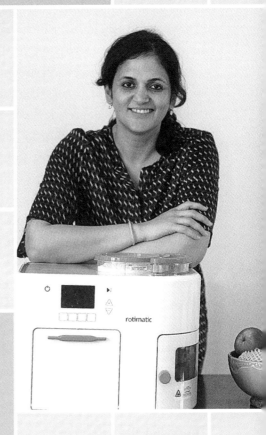

"In most industries, people follow norms. You need a disruptor to come in and change things."

Pranoti Nagarkar

Endowed with a scientific bent of mind, armed with a mechanical engineering degree from the National University of Singapore (NUS) — but a rebel at heart — Pranoti Nagarkar consciously channels her energy for the betterment of others. As a student living alone in Singapore, the daily struggle to prepare rotis (Indian flatbreads) motivated her to come up with the idea of making a kitchen appliance that would take the tedium out of the daily chore. Her invention, the Rotimatic, does just that without compromising on freshness, nutrition and taste.

It wasn't an easy journey. From conceptualizing the product to building several prototypes and finally creating that one machine that could cook a roti to perfection, Pranoti has come a long way. Husband Rishi Israni, who graduated from the School of Computing in NUS, worked on developing the software; he introduced artificial intelligence and IoT (Internet of Things) capabilities, making it possible to troubleshoot and upgrade the machine automatically and remotely.

The Rotimatic is a complicated machine involving several motors, sensors, moving parts and artificial intelligence that all come together to knead and roll the dough to churn out one roti a minute.

Through the whole process, Pranoti has authored 37 patents. The couple truly is the wind beneath each other's wings, bringing their expertise, strengths and working styles to lead Zimplistic, the company that manufactures Rotimatic, to success. Together, they have given the world an iconic product designed and made in Singapore.

Think global, act local
It was in 2008 when Pranoti seriously planted the seeds to turn her dream of making a roti-making machine to reality.

Her conviction in the product was extraordinarily strong and she was able to raise a tidy sum of money from crowdfunding, angel investors and the investment arm of the Economic Development Board of Singapore.

Together with an initial investment of $20,000 from her savings, the couple operated out of NUS Enterprise's start-up hub at Block 71 Ayer Rajah Industrial Estate. This was the ideal environment for them as they were surrounded by bright young entrepreneurs, engineers and software developers, all bubbling with ideas and enthusiasm to create something new. Within a year, Zimplistic won the Start-Up@Singapore business plan competition. There was no looking back.

"Singapore as a country is also a start-up success story," analogizes Pranoti. "Our pioneer leaders looked for best practices, every initiative was purpose-led, and Singaporeans are enjoying the fruits of what they built. Like Singapore, Zimplistic also started with a blank slate, and through dedication, focus and hard work has attained enviable success."

Zimplistic has an inspired and enthusiastic team that knows they have a winner on their hands and are willing to push it to greater heights. Dubbed "the best thing since sliced bread" by the *Wall Street Journal*, Rotimatic has been warmly welcomed in Singapore homes. Some F&B outlets have also taken to using the Rotimatic to increase productivity as what was previously done by hand is now being done by machine.

The first Rotimatic rolled out in 2015 and by the end of 2019, nearly 60,000 machines had been sold in 20 countries — all via online channels — and have impacted the lives of some 35,000 families.

Headquartered in Singapore, the focus at the Zimplistic office is on getting the job done rather than clocking office hours.

Conscious of the fact that she was making both the product and building the company from scratch, Pranoti put together an efficient team of youngsters to forge ahead. The success of Rotimatic has created jobs for over a hundred people and set a benchmark for other entrepreneurs.

"There is no racial discrimination in Singapore. It is a pure talent-based economy. We could dream big because of a strong network of friends and supporters, manufacturing talent and government support to a start-up," says Pranoti. It was overwhelming when in 2016, a young company like theirs was praised by Prime Minister Lee Hsien Loong during his National Day Speech.

Pranoti and Rishi both set remarkably high standards of excellence and remain unflustered by setbacks. Despite its success, the company was not financially sustainable and was sold to Light Ray Holdings in 2021. However, the management and operational teams remain intact.

Even with all that fame and success, they are not sitting back to enjoy the fruits of their labour but working hard to add new features and software updates to the machine. Their dream is to invent more robotic kitchen devices so that the kitchen of the future becomes automated.

Achieving big goals through tiny steps

Pranoti grew up in Pune, India and became a Singapore citizen in 2012. She was an ace National Cadet in India and the discipline and rigour of the training gave her the resilience she needed to face life's challenges. At the age of 16, she moved to Singapore on a scholarship granted by the Ministry of Education to further her studies at the National Junior College. Not only was she away from home, but as a scholarship holder, there was the added pressure of having to achieve academically. If her performance faltered, she would have been sent back. A focused and motivated person, Pranoti worked hard to settle down in her new environs.

Today many of her close friends are local Singaporeans. She enjoys the food here and often goes back to NUS for a taste of familiar fare. The initial struggles, she says, have made her a more adaptable person. "I think I am a success if I control my mind and my emotions. I measure success in terms of what impact my actions have on society. That is why if I spot a problem, my first reaction is to look for a solution," she adds.

Pranoti credits her stint at NUS for her love for technology. "I gained a lot of experience, the facilities are top-notch, and the faculty supportive which laid the foundation for my technological entrepreneurship journey."

Rotimatic has been a game-changer for her. She is often invited to give talks and share experiences. Youngsters approach her for advice on their journey.

A strong supporter of women's rights, Pranoti worked hard to be taken seriously in a male-dominated field. She encourages women to believe in themselves, to know they are important in influencing the next generation. Pregnancy and domestic matters should not be barriers to employment because women are efficient at multi-tasking and can contribute very meaningfully to society. As a young mother of two sons, she understands the difficulties of working and raising children, and allows her female staff to have the flexibility to work part-time or from home.

Pranoti is aware and conscious of herself and the world around her. Despite the tremendous pressure both at home and work, she is cheerful and outgoing and doesn't take herself too seriously. She calls herself "a work in progress" and admires people like

Mahatma Gandhi and Mother Teresa, who lived a simple life but left a profound legacy for the world.

For someone so young, Pranoti has a spiritual bent of mind and avoids materialism and frivolous talk. "We should develop a culture of helping others. The good thing about Singapore is that there is no pressure to conform. Singapore lets you be yourself. The government takes care of day-to-day issues so the residents can focus on bettering themselves and focus on the less fortunate," she says.

Pranoti believes Singaporeans should have more children as long as the reason for having them is right. "Kids take away the drudgery, ground us and are a de-stressor." As a family they relax by enjoying the outdoors, playing badminton, cycling and discovering hidden spots that make Singapore a garden city.

The journey so far has been exciting and Pranoti and Rishi are looking forward to the next chapter, happy in the knowledge that they pursued their dream and are enjoying the glory of it coming true.

INTEGRATING THROUGH COMMUNITY BONDING

"Through my volunteering activities I not only help the community, but I also inculcate good values in my kids and set an example for them and my students."

Dr Sun Guang Wen

From an introverted 19-year-old student who set foot in Singapore in 1997 to a lecturer at Republic Polytechnic, Dr Sun Guang Wen has come a long way. He is no longer the quiet, studious boy trying to find a foothold in a foreign land. The scientifically inspired youngster has achieved his goal of becoming a researcher and a teacher.

A desire for higher education brought Guang Wen from Nanjing, China to Singapore where he studied at the National University of Singapore (NUS), graduating first with a BSc in Biochemistry and then with a PhD in Microbiology and Immunology. The son of a retired school principal and a housewife, he was the first high school graduate in his immediate family. Even though his family valued education, financial pressures made many young people of his generation drop out early.

Appreciating the privileges

An understanding and appreciation for the privileges given to him by the Singapore government motivates him to give back to Singapore. He is now returning the favour by teaching the younger generation and indirectly supporting the future economy. A lecturer at the School of Applied Science at Republic Polytechnic for the last eight years, Guang Wen estimates that he must have interacted with over a thousand students during this time. His first batch of students have already joined the workforce and are contributing manifold to society both in Singapore and overseas.

He is proud to teach at the polytechnic and finds it particularly rewarding as he can help to shape the future of the many young students he meets. Some alumni keep in touch with him and witnessing his students' personal growth beyond the classroom gives him immense joy.

Around the time he completed his PhD in 2006, the Singapore government was pouring in huge amounts of money to set up centres for cutting-edge research. As a result, in many disciplines, Singapore is today among the top research centres in the world. Having lived here for over two decades, Guang Wen has seen first-hand how forward thinking the government is and how well its long-term plans align with its vision of Singapore. This, he believes, has helped the country move forward rapidly.

Guang Wen finds scientific research meaningful. "It's a privilege to discover new knowledge, and it is very fulfilling," he says. He believes that scientific development and discoveries drive the economy. "It is very important to continue to invest in R&D. The government's large investment in biomedical science for example has led to it becoming one of the pillars of Singapore's economy."

He fondly recollects a paper he published in 2005. Titled "Caspase-1 dependent macrophage death induced by *Burkholderia pseudomallei*", it brought to light breakthrough research in the field of bacterial infection and led to further study on the subject. "Indirectly, my team-mates and I contributed to a better understanding of bacterial infection disease, further helping scientists to understand the molecular mechanism of bacterial virulence," he says.

Thankfully, Republic Polytechnic gives him and other researchers the academic freedom as well as facilities and a reasonable budget to collaborate with industry and local and overseas researchers. "Science develops very fast and we will be left behind if we don't keep up," he says.

He is immensely grateful for receiving a scholarship from the Ministry of Education, which has allowed him to further his studies at NUS. While there has been criticism that these scholarships only benefitted overseas students, Guang Wen feels that in the long term, Singapore has also gained from the collective talents of the students as most of them have chosen to make Singapore their home and contribute to its progress. In addition, in an increasingly connected world it gives Singaporeans exposure to people from other countries.

He strongly believes that Singapore has brought out his hidden talents and broadened his experience.

Serving the community and reaping the benefits

Guang Wen took up citizenship in 2010. What makes him a true-blue Singaporean are his friends in his HDB neighbourhood, his ability to converse in Singlish and his adoption of a Singaporean way of life. He is comfortable living in the heartlands and working with grassroots leaders to help needy families. His children were born here and know no other home.

Home is in Ayer Rajah where in the initial years, he and his wife rented a flat. He regrets that because of his busy study schedule he could never devote time to community events. It was only in 2006, after he bought a flat in Teban Gardens, that Guang Wen truly sank roots into Singapore and became more socially active.

Guang Wen has volunteered as a grassroots leader with the People's Association (PA) since 2009. The PA has been instrumental in building a harmonious and cohesive society in Singapore. Intending to bring different segments of Singapore society together, it engages grassroots organizations to connect Singaporeans under one umbrella through social, cultural, educational and sporting activities.

Being a grassroots leader has given him many opportunities to meet more Singaporeans. "Every community event is attended by thousands of people. I would never have known them otherwise.

I have made friends and often go out with them for makan, jogging, dragon boating or other sports activities," adding that he has shed his shyness and now enjoys interacting with people.

Thanks to the government policy of allocating flats according to population ratio, he counts two Chinese, a Malay and an Indian family as his immediate neighbours. Over the years he has learnt to enjoy Malay and Indian cuisine and has become more culturally aware of each community's traditions. It is particularly useful, now that he is so actively involved in grassroots work. "If I am organizing an event, I think about the food restrictions of all communities and accordingly arrange for halal or vegetarian food."

He is particularly close to his Indian neighbour. They visit each other at home, exchange hong baos and cookies on auspicious occasions, and their children play together almost every day.

"Regardless of where you come from, the best way to forge bonds with your neighbours and the local community is through volunteering. It is very satisfying and helps you to integrate with the people living in the heartlands of Singapore," he says.

He is involved in the Community Emergency and Engagement Committees (C2E), which plays a supporting role to the Singapore Civil Defence Force and helps strengthen community resilience. As a C2E member, Guang Wen is trained and certified in first aid. He says this has made him more aware of his surroundings and alert to any situations that may arise where he can be of help.

He is also involved in the Community Development & Welfare Fund (CDWF), having held various roles (as assistant secretary, assistant treasurer and, currently, treasurer) for eight years. The CDWF assists needy and meritorious students in pursuing education, provides financial and social assistance to disadvantaged residents, and arranges welfare programmes and facilities for the promotion of social cohesion, racial harmony and civic responsibility. Helping those who need help makes him feel good. "On the outside, Singapore seems like a well-developed society with high income levels, but the truth is, there are a significant number of families who get left behind and need more help," explains Guang Wen.

He, along with the CDWF team at Ayer Rajah GRC, visits the elderly and families in need of help. Aid is not always monetary. They help to clean, repaint and repair homes, assisting wherever they feel they can help.

Working with ordinary Singaporeans has changed Guang Wen's life. "When people have nothing, they have gratitude. By helping others, I learnt the importance of family." An intangible benefit of all his activities is that from a young age, his two sons are evincing interest in what he does and sometimes are keen to get involved and help him. "I feel so good being able to help the less fortunate," says the self-confessed atheist.

For the last five years, Guang Wen has also been distributing food to the needy through a programme called Food Connect. He leads a team of volunteers to order rations in bulk and repack them for distribution. Rations such as rice, cooking oil and canned food are delivered every month to over a hundred families across all races.

To Guang Wen, integration is a natural need of man. Man cannot live in isolation. Over in Nanjing where he grew up, everyone knew everyone and all occasions whether happy or sad were commemorated together. These days, events held at community centres take him back to his growing-up days. "People come out of their houses and intermingle. We don't even realize how many people live around us and such events bring us together as Singaporeans, giving us a sense of belonging."

"Life would still have been good if he had lived in China but different," he reminisces. However, Singapore is home!

MIRRORING SINGAPORE'S SOUL THROUGH STORIES

"Imagination is only a small part of my skill as a writer, the rest is observation. My stories have themes that find resonance among readers because they are the stories of ordinary everyday Singaporeans."

Kamaladevi Aravindan

Mr K. Sarangapani, founder of *Tamil Murasu*, Singapore's only Tamil newspaper, called her the pride of Tamils after she was declared the winner of a Tamil literary competition. A Malayalee by birth, the 16-year-old proved her ability and knowledge of Tamil by reciting pieces of classical poetry to an overawed audience. This was one of the many victories which would become typical for the talented teenager who went on to carve a name for herself in the literary scene both in Singapore and Malaysia.

Today, the distinguished Tamil writer, now known as Kamaladevi Aravindan, is a recipient of several awards and remains one of the most prolific writers of her generation.

Born and brought up in Johor Bahru, Malaysia, Kamaladevi started writing at a young age. She regularly participated in competitions and often won books as prizes, which helped nurture her language skills. Her teachers would lend her Tamil books to read, spurring her interest in Tamil literature. They encouraged her by submitting her essays for publication in *Tamil Murasu*, launching her career as a writer.

Moving from strength to strength

Her marriage in 1972 brought Kamaladevi to Singapore. By then she was already an established and well-known writer. Juggling her home and writing stories for the newspaper, the young Kamaladevi quietly observed and absorbed the sights and sounds of daily life. A talent that she put to good use in her work.

At a time when there was no social media, she was not shy to reach out to and interact with established writers through letters, benefitting immensely from their guidance and advice.

Kamaladevi was always up for a challenge and recalls her delight when she received a letter from then Radio and Television

Singapore, asking if she could write original dramas and short stories for radio. She quickly accepted the offer even though it required a drastic shift in her writing style.

With their two little girls in tow, her husband would accompany her to the radio station. Her short plays were broadcast every Tuesday, and a serialized drama on Fridays. It required a lot of work, but she rose to the challenge. Her popularity among the Tamil community — her primary audience — soared. Television followed soon after and Kamaladevi never looked back.

Since she was also fluent in Malayalam, she started writing for Malayalam productions that were staged by the several Malayalee organizations here. In 1992, in a drama competition, she won Singapore's Best Playwright, Best Director and Best Author for the play *Silanthivala* (Spider Web).

Over a career spanning five decades, Kamaladevi has written over 300 radio dramas, 162 short stories, 18 stage plays and five books. Her books *Nuval* and *Karavu* are a compilation of short stories in Tamil and taught at the University of Malaya. Her short stories have also been published in India, Malaysia, USA and Switzerland, and translated into English and French, winning her much global acclaim.

In 2014, '*Mugadugal*' was chosen as the best short story at the Singapore Writers Festival. It was adapted and made into a film which went on to win three awards. The same year, *Nigazhkalayil Naan*', a story which traces her journey in the world of theatre, received the Jeyanthan Foundation Lifetime Playwright Award. Another short story *Soorya Grahana Theru* was featured in the National Arts Council's (NAC) short story publication *Fiction Singapore 2014*. She also won the Indian Muslim Association's Societal Literature Contributor Award in 2000.

The award-winning writer specializes in *Parikshartha* drama literature, which incorporates an experimental writing style. She spent six months in India training in this style of writing incorporating Tamil influences. Another attribute of her writing style is that she explores different facets of a problem, allowing the reader to arrive at their own solutions to the problem.

For the bubbly Kamaladevi, age is just a number. She taught herself to use the computer and has mastered typing in the Tamil font. She blogs in Tamil and does not let technology impede her literary output.

She humbly gives credit to her mentors from the Tamil literary community, her colleagues at work and the opportunities that were afforded to her, which guided her along on a journey to success.

A people's person

Kamaladevi's stories are not a figment of her imagination but stem from her own experiences. "I am a sensitive person," she confides. "I talk to people, I observe, I empathize, I feel the other person's pain. Life inspires me and it is real-life incidents that I write about. My readers identify with them."

In the early days, she mostly wrote love stories. Young girls would read them and show their appreciation by shyly running up to her and pressing a mango or a durian from their garden into her hands.

She has since gravitated towards writing about the harsher realities of life. Once an idea strikes, she unhesitatingly speaks to the relevant people to get an insider understanding of the problem. There were times when people found it strange to see her engaged in an animated conversation with a sweeper or walking around in a red-light area or visiting a mental asylum. Not one to be deterred, she churned out story after story about marginalized and deprived members of society. *Karavu*, an anthology of short stories, speaks about underprivileged Singaporeans, drawing attention to the need to be humanitarian to enable them to transform their lives.

Her work is so popular that she was once stopped in Tekka Market in Serangoon and hugged by an old lady who liked a story she had written. Even today, people on the streets recognize and congratulate her on her work that so beautifully captures the joys and woes of everyday life in Singapore.

As a nation of immigrants, Kamaladevi stresses the need to be proficient in one's mother tongue as it connects us to our roots. "We cannot forget where we came from, as that makes us who we are," she says passionately.

Bringing alive Singapore's kampung past

Kamaladevi's latest novel *Sembawang* is currently making waves. It is her first attempt at writing historical fiction. Written in Tamil and set against the backdrop of real-life incidents that happened in Sembawang where she arrived as a young bride, it seeks to showcase the historical and vanishing aspects of life as it was then. It has been translated into English by her daughter Anitha Devi Pillai, an acclaimed writer herself, giving it wider readership and appreciation.

"Sembawang was then referred to as Little Kerala, because of the large population of Keralites living there," Kamaladevi reminisces. "We had many Chinese and Malay neighbours and lived a contented life. It was kampung spirit at its best as we learnt from each other, shared our joys and sorrows, celebrated festivals together and helped each other. When I was pregnant, they would pass me pickled or raw mangoes. They would take care of my girls when I had to run errands. If anyone died, irrespective of the race, we would all be there to console the bereaved family."

With its plethora of human emotions and relationships, *Sembawang* tugs at the heartstrings of Singaporeans. It is the story of a time and life that she remembers with nostalgia.

A proud Singaporean since 1990, Kamaladevi says she is confident that the government has the best interests of the citizens in mind and that helps her enjoy a stress-free life. The NAC has regularly supported her work, and she has represented Singapore in book fairs, writers' festivals and conferences both in Singapore and overseas.

"Singapore has given me the confidence to stand on my own two feet, travel to foreign countries alone and share the stage with Tamil literary luminaries," says Kamaladevi.

A lifelong learner, she has plans to go overseas and study Shakespeare's works. Her mind is brimming with ideas and incidents. The sky is the limit, and her best is yet to come.

CREATING
A NATION
BY DESIGN

"A nation that does not think
and question degrades over time
The youth must start questionin
the status quo which
is particularly important for
Singapore to move forward.
Community engagement can
be a powerful platform to forge
greater bonds across society.
It's a duty we all share."

Larry Yeung

Upon completing his National Service, Larry Yeung was taken aback when in 2010, he received a letter asking him to choose between being a Singaporean or a British Overseas Citizen. He was only three years old when his family moved to Singapore from Hong Kong and they had been Singapore citizens since then. His parents never revealed to him that he had dual citizenship because they saw the merit in serving a country which had offered them the best possible home that any family could ask for.

Not that Larry would have it any other way. Singapore is the only home he has known and he has always felt like a true homegrown Singaporean. He therefore opted to retain his Singapore citizenship.

The young architecture trained designer is the executive director of Participate in Design (P!D), a non-profit organization engaged in helping neighbourhoods and public institutions design community-owned spaces. "We are a design company, but the work that we do has social value and benefits the community," explains Larry. He has been working together with grassroots organizations, educational institutions and statutory boards to develop a creative approach to encourage residents to participate in designing the neighbourhoods they live in.

Community engagement

The desire to work with the community did not come by chance. A strong believer in building engaged and empowered communities, his interest in social issues was stoked during a project while he was a student of Architecture at the National University of Singapore. The theme of his master's thesis was on creating a sustainable neighbourhood in rental housing estates and revitalizing them using participatory design.

After completing his studies, he worked in the private sector for two years and was part of the team tasked with enhancing the National Orchid Garden as part of the Singapore Botanic Gardens' UNESCO Heritage site bid.

Since his interests have always been social and community-centric, Larry decided to quit his job and join P!D. The organization was founded in 2013 by some of his seniors at the university on the belief that it is the stakeholders who should have a say in what they would like to see in their neighbourhood. The founders felt that even though Singapore has beautiful public places, many of them were underutilized or littered. "We started questioning why this was happening and realized that people feel no ownership of their surroundings. As we become more educated, it is natural for people to demand to have a say in the environment where they live," says Larry.

One of their early projects was 'Welcome to Our Back Yard', in collaboration with the MacPherson Citizen's Consultative Committee. Through a series of participatory programmes, stakeholders were involved in sharing ideas for transforming an underutilized piece of land into a more utilitarian place in accordance with the desire of the public. The project received a lot of good publicity and became an example of how residents could come together to co-create a design space. It was a classic example of rethinking the whole process of design. The idea caught on and these days it has become almost a prerequisite for public places to seek the opinion of residents. Larry feels that it was not just empowering for the people but very fulfilling for him as well.

"P!D was one of the pioneers of this movement in Singapore. Residents are given a chance to express their ideas and we were there to help them present these ideas to the experts and authorities for their consideration," explains Larry. Previously, he would design for the public without understanding what they wanted. In his present job, the process is very different and exciting, and even though he took a significant pay cut to join them, it's a decision he has never regretted, as he now does something that makes a difference to society.

Another worthy project was one where he had to design a community kitchen for a senior activity centre. It was a huge challenge, as he had to work closely with the elderly residents and find ways to encourage them to share their vision and expectations. This he managed to do successfully through various activities designed to break the ice. It also helped that he could speak Cantonese, Mandarin and a smattering of Malay — and the older folks eventually opened up to him. The success of this project highlighted to Larry the value of participatory design. "The seniors felt empowered that they could contribute to the community at large and it made them realize their self-worth," he says.

He sleeps well at night because he finds value in what he does. "I am championing how our civil service can look at the needs of the public in a manner that will satisfy them. We must constantly challenge ourselves to add value and showcase new ways to do things. It's a way the nation can improve," says Larry.

A home built on hopes and dreams

For Larry, the presence of family and friends makes Singapore home. He lives with his parents in an HDB flat in Punggol and hopes that the Singaporean virtue of being filial to one's parents and elderly family members and having close family bonds will be sustained in the future as well. He travels abroad for work and vacation, but the joy of landing at Changi Airport and the feeling of homecoming is, for him, incomparable.

Living in a housing board flat in the Balestier area during his youth helped connect him with the heartlanders. He grew up doing what many Singaporean boys of his age do — playing at the void decks and neighbourhood playgrounds with kids from different races and religions.

It was his desire to be one with the other students in his neighbourhood school that prompted Larry to try eating local food. He enjoyed curry so much that he would often pester his mother to cook it at home. It was his first step towards integrating with Singapore society. He would often share with his parents what he learnt about other cultures and faiths from his friends and happily takes partial credit for teaching them the local traditions.

Today Larry is Singaporean to the core and is at home with speaking Singlish. He rattles off names of his favourite foods like roti prata, laksa, mee siam and Hokkien mee, and has brought a Singapore flavour to his extended family in Hong Kong by teaching them how to 'chope' seats at hawker centres.

In 2020, Larry was involved in the Citizens' Workgroup for the 'Singapore Citizenship Journey' project, which was organized in support of the Singapore Together Movement. As an immigrant himself, he feels more can be done to integrate new citizens. He hopes through this project, they can come up with a meaningful journey for new citizens, one that is more authentic and showcases the real Singapore, similar to what he experienced when he came here. "We should display the Singapore values of resilience and helpfulness, translating them into practice," he says passionately.

For Larry, success means making a difference, however small, and leaving the world a better place. He is hopeful that his generation will carve a new path forward. "We have room for more love and acceptance of different lifestyles and belief systems. We just need to embrace differences and be less polarized so that in the Singapore of the future, we can talk about our successes but are also willing to discuss our differences and work as a nation to address them. That is the Singapore of my dreams."

ROBOTICS AND THE SMART NATION

"Robotics can potentially play a more crucial role in improving the quality of our lives. My vision and dream are for the robot to be the ultimate companion and communication tool, especially as we grow older, and to live in a utopic world where humans and robots work together to maximize efficiency and make life more meaningful for all of us."

Dr Marcelo H Ang Jr

The mention of robots brings to mind sci-fi movies featuring mechanized figures that look and act like humans and speak in a weird, high-pitched voice. In real life, robots are machines that are being increasingly used in industries such as healthcare, agriculture, construction, transport, military and space — with the aim of assisting humans in doing things faster, safely, efficiently and at less cost. Dr Marcelo H Ang Jr, Professor in the Department of Mechanical Engineering at the National University of Singapore (NUS), is one of the pioneers in the robotics scene in Singapore. He confidently looks forward to the day, in the not too distant future, when driverless vehicles and personal robotic assistants will become commonplace.

On the right track

Autonomous Vehicles (AVs), according to Marcelo, who is also the Acting Director of the Advanced Robotics Centre at NUS, are an ecological and practical solution to urban transportation woes especially in places like Singapore which have limited land space. AVs provide 'Mobility on Demand', which will eliminate the need to own vehicles as commuters will be able to call up vehicles of different sizes and for different needs as and when required. They can prove to be safer and more reliable on roads.

As part of the Smart Nation Initiative, launched by Prime Minister Lee Hsien Loong in 2014, Marcelo and his team conducted the first deployment of AVs in Singapore and unveiled self-driving, four-wheeled electric vehicles which are especially useful for people with mobility issues. This project was in collaboration with the Singapore-MIT Alliance for Research and Technology.

In healthcare, Marcelo envisions a world where the sick can recuperate at home with the help of a robotic assistant, to help them exercise or support them during toilet visits. In hospitals, robots could take over the back-breaking job of turning patients over and relieve the nurses from routine and repetitive duties such as taking and recording of a patient's vitals. If robots were available today, they could conduct swab tests for the Covid-19 virus, thereby minimizing human contact and transmission of the virus. The possibilities according to Marcelo are unlimited and exciting.

The professor likens a robot to a cellphone with arms and legs to assist us in our daily routine. "Something you can't do without and which makes our life better in a million small ways. The human brain has a lot of potential which should not be wasted in jobs that are demeaning, degrading, dirty and dangerous," elaborates Marcelo, whose research spans robotics, automation, computer control and artificial intelligence.

Robots have been successfully deployed in factories and structured environments. Marcelo would like to bring this technology into our unstructured, human environment. Early on in his career, Marcelo developed the first-ever robotic system for ship welding that did not require learning the robotics programming language. His goal is to develop easy-to-use robotic systems, which are as simple to use as other everyday consumer devices.

He sits on the Advisory Council of the World Robot Olympiad and is the founding chairman of the Singapore Robotic Games, a competition that aims to inculcate a robotics culture among youngsters, exercise their creativity, and encourage the creation and use of robots in everyday life. Despite limited resources and minimal costs, the annual event has managed to gain world-wide attention, thanks to the efforts of Marcelo and his dedicated team of volunteers.

A smart city with smart capabilities

Marcelo grew up in Manila, Philippines where he did a double degree in Mechanical and Industrial Engineering. In 1981 during his first job with Intel Philippines, he had access to the then state-of-the-art IBM PC, which sparked his interest in computers and opened his mind to their potential. While pursuing his master's in Mechanical Engineering at the University of Hawaii, one of his projects revolved around using robots for sugarcane harvesting. Since robotics is a mix of mechanical and electrical engineering and computer science, his educational interests naturally led him to this research area. He went on to complete his PhD in Electrical Engineering from the University of Rochester in New York in 1988.

His teaching stint at the University of Rochester was cut short when he was offered a job at NUS. During his interview with Professor Tommy Koh, then Singapore's ambassador to the US, Prof Koh shared Singapore's plans to be a smart nation — an idea much ahead of its time. He believed that robotics was the key to achieving that goal. Marcelo was won over by Prof Koh's sincerity and warmth, and he moved to Singapore within a few months. He had never been to Singapore, but was already dreaming of playing a part in making it a smart city.

The year was 1989, and Marcelo realized that the work culture here was very different from what he was used to in the US. Troubled by the fact that he did not have access to his laboratory 24/7, the go-getter created the first card access system in his lab in NUS so that he and others keen on working after office hours could enter and exit when they pleased. Today, this facility is common in most workplaces.

Marcelo likes to apply his research to real-life situations and has multiple patents and publications to his name. He is an elected member of the Institute of Electrical and Electronics Engineers' Robotics and Automation Society, a very prestigious international society for robotics scientists, professionals, educators and practitioners.

Since 1989, he has been closely involved with a programme targeted at junior college students to attract them towards a career in research in science and technology. At NUS, the academic gets the opportunity to interact with bright students. He feels pride when they do well and reach out to him, sometimes after decades, to inform him about their achievements. He rattles off names of well-known engineers, budding entrepreneurs and scientists who were once his students and is heartened that he, in his small way, had a hand in setting them on the right paths. He revels in making others happy and positively impacting their lives gives him joy. His enthusiasm for teaching, innovating and consulting in his areas of interest keeps him rejuvenated.

Furthermore, he thoroughly enjoys how Singapore embraces technology and harvests its benefits.

Marcelo, who along with his family took up Singapore citizenship in 2008, enjoys the comfortable lifestyle that Singapore affords him. He appreciates simple things such as the easy access to banks and supermarkets on public holidays, weekends and weeknights. Plus, the red Singapore passport makes travelling a breeze which is particularly useful as he has a lot of work-related travelling to do. In all aspects — except the humid weather — he finds Singapore perfect.

And as he now feels he belongs here, he also believes he has the right to hope that his fellow Singaporeans will become more caring. "How we treat people shows if we are a First World country. A country's soul should not need campaigns to be politer and kinder. Instead, we should all live by example," says the father of three sons. His elder son is currently working, and the younger two, having completed their national service, are pursuing higher studies.

For the Filipino of Chinese descent, one advantage of coming to Singapore has been the reconnection to his Hokkien roots. The island nation's multiracial society has made him more aware of other cultures and more understanding of the sensibilities of his non-Chinese neighbours and colleagues.

In real life as in robotics, Marcelo sees infinite possibilities. He paints a picture of a future when innovation in robotics will lead to creations such as an autonomous vehicle made in Singapore, with an arm to do deliveries, collect domestic refuse, trim trees, and even take to the air to inspect tall buildings. The sky is the limit for Marcelo, as he devotes himself towards harnessing technology to create a better life for his fellow Singaporeans.

FORGING A MUSICAL PATHWAY TO INTEGRATION

"When my former colleagues and friends in Europe hear a new music composition that I have written, they say they hear Asian influences. Strangely I do not hear them. My journey in Singapore has led me to a continuous flow of rich discoveries in which I have internalized Asian musical influences."

Dr Robert Casteels

The first concert to mark Singapore's 50th year of independence in January 2015 took place on the Shaw Foundation Symphony Stage at the Botanic Gardens. The audience marvelled at the Malay, Chinese, Indian and European percussion instruments. This magical blend fittingly celebrated Singapore's multicultural and multi-ethnic identity. The concert was the brainchild of composer, conductor, educator and pianist Dr Robert Casteels. According to him, far from paying lip service to politically correct interracial representation, he wanted to speak to the hearts of the audience and hoped the different races would appreciate each other's musical heritage.

Robert has contributed much to Singapore's music scene. He has served as the Dean of the Faculty of Performing Arts at LASALLE-SIA College of the Arts; as Music Director of the Singapore National Youth Orchestra; as Founding Artistic Director & Resident Conductor of the Philharmonic Winds; as Associate-in-Residence (Special Projects) and Music Director of the National University of Singapore's choir, wind and guitar orchestras; and as guest conductor of the Singapore Symphony Orchestra and the Yong Siew Toh Conservatory of Music (these are just a few of the many orchestras he has worked with).

He has been a jury member at various competitions and is often invited to sit on the board of art and education committees. A regular performer at concerts, Robert has written several hundred musical works both within the strict parameters of classical European music tradition as well as fusion pieces combining the best of what Eastern tradition has to offer. In 2004, he was awarded a doctorate for his thesis on gamelan and contemporary music.

Singapore, his new home

Robert grew up in Belgium and it was his mother, an amateur pianist, who first noticed his talent and enrolled him in music school. Thereafter he attended both the Flemish and French Royal Music Conservatories in Brussels. Honing his talent further in London and New York, Robert returned to Europe to carve out a successful career for himself. In 1995, while conducting in Melbourne, he was offered a high-profile academic position in Singapore. For someone who did not know much about Singapore, he soon fell in love with the island nation. Working at LASALLE College was like being in a colony of artists. He felt encouraged to find his fit and is grateful for the opportunities to achieve his dreams.

Robert says he could identify with Singapore because, "like Belgium, Singapore is a small country surrounded by large countries. Singaporeans, like Belgians, are pragmatic and modest. They go about their lives, work hard and end up achieving more than their neighbours."

One of the things about Singapore that surprised him was the many Chinese, Malay and Indian food stalls in schools and food courts. He thought they were an efficient social equalizer. So too was the way festivals of the different races are celebrated, each with the same respect for the other, and he enjoyed attending Thaipusam and Chinese New Year festivities. All this impressed him for in Singapore, social and racial harmony are not hollow words but a precious reality.

Stay or go back? That was the conundrum Robert, like most immigrants, faced in his early years. However, it soon became clear that Singapore was where he wanted to be. Robert and his family took up citizenship in 2007.

"As long as I was a permanent resident and worked in this country, I was grateful for the privilege of living and working here, and I would never criticize nor comment. The moment I became a citizen, my perception changed. I have a stake and therefore I have an opinion. I began standing up for Singapore and defending Singapore if the occasion warranted. I interact with the Member of Parliament in my constituency and participate in community events. My opinion counts to the same degree as anyone else born here, that's important," he says.

Robert sent his children to local schools to help them integrate better. His initial efforts at keeping them in touch with their mother tongue, Flemish, were soon put on the back burner as they picked up the local lingo. Both his children speak fluent Mandarin and are Singaporean in their choice of friends, language and food habits. His son has completed National Service and works full time, while his daughter is married to a Singaporean Chinese and settled here.

Bringing together musical notes harmoniously

Singapore's music scene has evolved since Robert came here over a quarter of a century ago. Today, facilities for the performing arts are superior to what one may find in many European countries. Over the years, several superbly maintained world-class concert halls have been built. The music scene however has become competitive to the point where supply exceeds demand. "Among so many talented musicians, it's a fight to get an audience," says Robert. "Singapore has the resources and goes all out to get the best of what is available, and yet has the maturity to do a U-turn if things don't go as planned," he says.

Even though he was used to the grand canvas of European music, he never felt constricted in Singapore. A whole other genre of fusion music became Robert's focus. He plunged headlong into understanding the various styles of music that Asia has to offer. He has learnt enough about Chinese and Indian music to be able to understand and appreciate them, and has successfully brought together, for example, the violin, Indian veena and Indonesian gamelan to create music. He often creates multidisciplinary works, combining western and eastern instruments with computer-generated sounds and images. "In Europe, I would be hard-pressed to find so many musicians playing instruments of different cultures. I am constantly growing artistically and that keeps me excited," says Robert.

When it comes to conducting music by maestros like Bach, Beethoven or Debussy, Robert considers himself to be an uncompromising and humble servant of tradition. But when he creates new music, he is not duty-bound to follow past rules. That is where his true talent lies. "I avoid performing in concerts that box me up. I choose the flute of a particular culture, not for its cultural affiliation, but for its timbral possibilities. In music, colour is called timbre."

Regardless of race, language or religion, music of all cultures throughout all times expresses the same type of emotions. "Obviously, I don't claim to fully understand the finer aspects of Asian musical instruments," confesses Robert. "Instead, I explain my ideas to the musicians. They are the experts in their field and know how to realize that idea on their instrument."

Inside the mind of a musician

Singapore is possibly the only country where you can find nature thriving in an urban setting. Robert has studied bird song and created musical pieces incorporating sounds of birds, insects, frogs, even rain and thunder.

Robert also believes that every artist has a social responsibility. He has conducted, performed and organized concerts in prisons and hospitals and for charities and fundraising galas.

He is critical of parental *kiasuism*, which subjects children to money making examination systems (students perform a few choice pieces over and over to collect certificates). He questions the pedagogical value of such an approach and believes it can turn many youngsters away from classical music.

"I hope I have contributed to Singapore. Singapore has certainly enriched me. No point pretending to act more local than the locals. There is no shame in being different. I will always remain grateful and appreciative towards Singapore," says Robert. "When I observe some Europeans I knew 25 years ago, still playing the same type of music, I am relieved I stepped out of my comfort zone and enlarged my horizons."

In 2001, Robert became the youngest recipient and the second musician ever to receive the prestigious Christoffel Plantin Prize, the Flemish government's highest award for cultural achievements, in recognition of his contribution to cross-cultural research. Among the many awards he has received, Robert treasures this the most as it is bestowed to Flemish people living outside of Flanders, the Dutch-speaking area of Belgium.

When nostalgia hits, he remembers the colours of autumn in his native Belgium and tries to plan his trips back home accordingly. At other times, the smells and sounds of the tropical rain in Singapore more than make up for it.

A HEART AND SOUL THAT BEATS FOR SINGAPORE

Despite differences in ethnicity, religion and culture, we live together as one people, with a harmony that is remarkable — always looking to help one another and serve the country."

Jaspreet Chhabra, PBM

Jaspreet Singh Chhabra is a content man. He has shouldered the responsibility of being the eldest son of his parents, helped his friends whenever required and risen to the top of his career. In spite of the trials and tribulations that he faced in his early years, he still feels that his has been a wonderful and satisfying journey. Jaspreet now finds peace in serving society in any way he can.

In 1997, after nearly 21 years in the Indian Merchant Navy, Jaspreet was offered a shore job as a marine manager in a company located in Singapore. It was an opportunity to put his knowledge of the shipping industry to good use by overseeing the marine operations of the company and conducting safe, productive and cost-effective cargo operations.

Another reason for the move was that in the course of his previous job, Jaspreet had been visiting the island nation on and off and felt that Singapore would provide a safe haven for his wife and two young children.

Jaspreet, who hails from Jullundur, India, currently helms the global freight operations of a major trading company. Well-versed with every facet of his work, he has vast experience on various seafaring vessels and is proud of his commitment to operational excellence.

A life lived on the principles of humanitarianism and volunteerism

Singapore is home to many cultures, ethnicities and nations, and that diversity, feels Jaspreet, is its strength. The government has created an environment where people of every race and religion are welcomed and made to feel secure.

Jaspreet, who took up citizenship in 2007, admires the government's policy of multiculturalism, where no race or culture is coerced into conforming to other identities. As a result, cohesion has been maintained in society.

For the devout Sikh, the multiracial society of Singapore aligns with his personal religious beliefs as Guru Nanak, the founder of Sikhism, in his teachings, emphasized the equality of all human beings, irrespective of caste, religion or social status.

As a member of the Inter-Racial and Religious Confidence Circle, he visits churches, mosques and other places of worship to understand the teachings of different religions and to rally communities to stand together especially in times of crisis.

Jaspreet currently serves as the Chairman of the Silat Road Sikh Temple, one of the larger gurudwaras (Sikh temple) in Singapore. The temple serves food daily to about 1,000 individuals from all communities without discrimination.

Growing up in India, he was influenced by his family's observance of *sewa* (service) at the local gurudwara, which instilled in him a desire to serve the community. Not long after arriving here, he became a member of the Gurudwara Sahib in Yishun and devoted his leisure time to volunteering there. Apart from serving food, washing utensils and cleaning the premises, Jaspreet looked into the maintenance and financial aspects of the temple and had the honour of being its secretary for 10 years.

He notes that even today, the gurudwara sends *langar* (community meal) to prison inmates and provides counselling for them. Their philanthropy is not limited to the Sikh community. Residents of The Ramakrishna Mission home receive *langar* once a week. During the Covid-19 pandemic, he was actively involved in serving packets of food and distributing dry provisions to other Sikh temples; Annalakshmi, a vegetarian restaurant where volunteers cook and patrons pay what they want; and charities like Willing Hearts.

Jaspreet is a committee member of the Central Sikh Gurudwara Board, which oversees several organizations such as the Youth Sikh Association and the Sikh Welfare Council.

He reaches out to youngsters and shares his experiences and knowledge with them, encouraging them to keep healthy, stay out of trouble and serve society according to the tenets of their faith. Jaspreet strongly favours inducting the youth in programmes that make them aware of the value of hard work. "Our youth are our future and they have to conserve what our forefathers have created. In the time to come, there could be business tensions, financial crises, or uncertain political situations in the region. Our youth should learn to value money and develop healthy habits," he says.

The Sikh Welfare Council looks after needy Sikh families, organizes visits to the homes of the elderly, and provides bursaries, tuitions and rations to those who will benefit from them.

Jaspreet can't stress enough on the value of volunteering. "Volunteering makes you humble. If we do anything for personal gain, it is not volunteering but selfishness. If we want to be successful and have a feeling of satisfaction, then we should serve society without any hope of gain," says the soft-hearted disciplinarian.

Sikhs are easily identified because of their distinctive turbans. However, many people are not aware of Sikhism and so the community makes an effort to educate people about their religion. They welcome students to their temples where they observe religious prayers and partake in *langar*. About 50 schools visit the gurudwaras annually. Jaspreet hopes these visits will help develop a healthy understanding of Sikhism and recognition that Sikhs welcome all faiths with open arms and are always looking to serve humanity.

Every bit helps

A humble, principled person, Jaspreet is one who doesn't give up easily. He credits his teachers and parents for moulding him to be the person that he is today. His school back in Jullundur used to provide food and water to the needy. Students took upon themselves the task of keeping the school clean and in so doing learnt the important lesson of dignity of labour.

It was during a chance meeting with Dr Tan Boon Wan and Dr Lee Bee Wah, both Members of Parliament from Nee Soon South GRC, that he was persuaded to join the Residents Committee as a volunteer. This opened up avenues for interaction with people of other races. Early on he had worked to secure a space at the local community centre where the elderly could get together and interact. Jaspreet slowly began to understand the local culture. "I realized that we were all working towards the same goal, the progress of Singapore, and that everyone had a good heart and wanted the best for Singapore," explains Jaspreet.

He also arranged for the needy to be provided with books and financial help. As the chairman for the Waterfront@ Khatib Neighbourhood Committee, his focus is always to help academically inclined students in need of financial support. He himself regularly donates money towards the bursaries. "My whole motivation is to share my pie with the needy and see their smiling faces whilst keeping a low profile," says the man whose family in his growing-up years was not very financially secure, making him aware of how a little help at the right time can go a long way.

Jaspreet credits his wife for supporting him every step of the way. Despite being highly educated herself, she uncomplainingly focused on their home and kids, even finding time to volunteer whenever and wherever possible. She currently teaches at the

Punjabi school where the Punjabi language is taught as a second language to students from kindergarten to A-Levels. At the same time, students are also made aware of their cultural heritage, inculcating in them a sense of respect for their inherited legacy. His family, he says, is his strength that keeps him anchored when waters become rough.

He has a message for newcomers to Singapore too. "People come here and want to make it their home because they are aware it is safe, but it will only remain so if we all continue to follow rules and avoid creating disharmony. The country will then welcome you with open arms," he says.

Singapore attracts and retains talent and Jaspreet is a shining example of this, having been awarded the Pingat Bakti Masyarakat in 2018 for his service to society, inspiring him even more to continue to contribute his time and resources for voluntary work.

"I love Singapore," says Jaspreet. "It has been a home for my children, the government works well, and there is peace and cohesiveness in society." Even though he goes back to India regularly to meet his parents, he is always in a hurry to come back as his heart belongs to Singapore.

CREATING CONNECTIONS BETWEEN SINGAPOREANS AND NATURE

"We all appreciate greenery, but we need to love the wildlife that comes with it as well. You can't love a butterfly but hate the caterpillar."

Gan Cheong Weei

The roots of Gan Cheong Weei's fondness for nature lie in his childhood in Penang, Malaysia. Growing up in the pre-Internet era, nature was an integral part of his life. After school, he would catch spiders and fish or look for caterpillars. His home was surrounded by fruit trees and the impressionable Cheong Weei was exposed to a variety of plants, triggering in him an enduring commitment towards nature.

Cheong Weei arrived in Singapore in 1983 to further his studies in Civil Engineering at the National University of Singapore (NUS). He missed the natural setting of his home, and it was only after he had graduated and become more comfortable in the Singapore milieu that he once again turned his attention to his first love — nature.

"I saw a newspaper cutting about nature walks," he recalls and soon joined a butterfly interest group under the aegis of the Nature Society. It was made up of likeminded people with similar interests and hobbies. "We exchanged experiences, asked questions and learnt from one another. Books were expensive and not easily available so that group was our classroom," says the passionate lepidopterist. Looking back 25 years later, he says the original group is still there and still as passionate about what they do.

Being the change he wished to see in the world

"Singapore may be a concrete jungle but compared to other countries, green areas here are very accessible and play a significant role in the ecosystem. We all have a role to play, whether big or small," explains Cheong Weei. He has been an active volunteer with the National Parks Board, Nature Society Singapore (NSS) as well as the Malayan Nature Society.

The veteran butterfly watcher created the NSS Nature Field Guide for butterflies and dragonflies so that members have an affordable, compact and colourful guide to help them identify these creatures.

Cheong Weei is also deeply passionate about information technology. Improved smartphones gave him the idea of creating a mobile field guide for butterflies and birds for NSS in 2014. The app has helped both the novice who wants to identify the creatures and the expert who wants to make notes and keep records.

It is little wonder that he was the Chairperson of the Butterfly and Insect Group from 2008 to 2012. A sub-group of NSS, its expert members are enthusiastic nature lovers who, apart from research, volunteer their time to conduct talks and tours for the public.

"Birds and insects don't live on their own; we cannot remove one and expect the other to survive. Nature is a whole ecosystem depending on each other for survival," says Cheong Weei.

He adds, "Sometimes we grow plants because of their aesthetics but if they are non-native, they may become invasive and exert unintended ecological effects on the local ecosystem." As different plants play different roles, diversity is important and NSS works closely with government and non-government organizations to plant more native and diverse plants to help maintain the fragile balance in nature.

Additionally, Cheong Weei is involved in Environmental Impact Assessment projects for lepidoptera ecology in Singapore. His knowledge and research contributes towards fact-based conservation. Like many NSS members, he is a volunteer in the area of his expertise. "You cannot protect what you don't know exists. Moths and butterflies are indirect indicators of the biodiversity of the area where they are found," explains Cheong Weei, who is a civil engineer by profession.

He gives the example of the Common Rose, the national butterfly of Singapore. It is a threatened species as the host plant on which its caterpillar feeds was removed in the early days. Today this plant is being reintroduced in an effort to provide suitable breeding and feeding areas for the butterfly.

Cheong Weei has co-authored *Marvellous Moths of Fraser's Hill*, a 258-page book which describes more than 600 species of moths found in Fraser's Hill in Pahang, Malaysia as well as Singapore. The book is the fruit of more than a decade of moth-watching and showcases the amazing variety and diversity of moths in the two countries.

Cheong Weei also manages the Singapore Moths project on iNaturalist, a global citizen science platform run by the California Academy of Sciences and the National Geographic Society. The project was started in 2014 to harness the power of mobile phones, the Internet and the public, to record moths found in Singapore. After eight years, more than 300 people have contributed close to 6,000 sightings totalling over 670 species. He couldn't have done it himself, says Cheong Weei who took up Singapore citizenship in 2012.

Making a difference

Cheong Weei is an optimist at heart and does not believe in looking back and regretting. "Look ahead. As long as we are around, we can make a difference," says the father of three daughters.

He is also an advisor to the Alexandra Hospital Butterfly Trail, the Butterfly Trail@Orchard, the Butterfly Garden at Changi Airport, several schools and gardens. Cheong Weei explains that the presence of butterflies make patients feel good. They also serve an educational purpose, exposing the younger generation to nature. "They must experience nature first hand. Once they are aware, it will make them curious and ignite an interest to explore. At least a few will become passionate and help protect nature," he says.

For Cheong Weei, volunteering is a good way to get people involved. It is a 'less commitment, more flexible' option without the pressure of meeting targets. This encourages more people to contribute, resulting in a lot of potential for innovation and permanent engagement.

Even in the condominium where he lives, Cheong Weei proactively ensured that green spaces were retained and plants and fruit trees planted to support birds, moths and butterflies. Sometimes squirrels and birds beat the residents to harvesting the fruits, but the nature lover says they need food too. "It cannot be about us, we are just a small part of a bigger picture," he adds.

He regrets that "our native animals are facing a lot of survival challenges like global warming, but habitat loss due to urban development is especially devastating and several species of animals are now extinct or endangered."

In the belief that even small gardens can have collective impact, Cheong Weei has created a miniature garden in his apartment with a large variety of plants. Dinner is in the balcony, surrounded by nature. Birds, butterflies and moths visit, attracted to plants specially grown for this purpose.

His is a hobby that takes up his weekends and spare time. He tries to focus on areas which have not been surveyed before, often spending nights away from home looking out for moths. His wife joins him whenever she can. It's tough as they get bitten by insects and covered in mud, and are exposed to the heat, rain and unpredictable weather of Singapore. The reward is in the opportunity to discover lesser-known creatures and record them for posterity, secure in the knowledge that there is a place in Singapore where they are alive and thriving.

His wish for Singapore is to have more accessible green areas inhabited with native animals and insects, so that various species that call Singapore home become more visible. "If we don't manicure too much, wildlife will thrive. Singaporeans need to be more accommodating and accepting. We need to work closely and collaborate with the government to develop a forest within the city."

IT STARTED WITH RAINCOATS!

"Any civilized society has to be empathetic.
Migrant workers are an essential
workforce. They benefit the country,
and we must integrate them and create
an inclusive society."

Dipa Swaminathan

While most of us look forward to going home after a hard day's work, celebrate festivals by buying expensive gifts for our families and enjoy the comforts of daily life, there is a community in Singapore that spends years on end away from their families, working hard to build the houses that we live in and maintain the infrastructure that keeps this country running. These are our often-overlooked foreign migrant workers.

Wanting to find ways to better their lives and make them feel at home in Singapore is Dipa Swaminathan. The Harvard educated corporate and commercial lawyer did just that and started the social initiative, ItsRainingRaincoats (IRR).

A platform for engagement

It all started in 2014 when driving home from work, Dipa saw two road cleaners caught in a thunderstorm. Moved by their plight and helplessness, she took them home. Over a change of clothes, hot drinks, food, and a little bit of coaxing, they shared their woes with her.

Not one to sit still, and endowed with a strong sense of justice, Dipa gave them her phone number in case they faced any problems in the future. The matter didn't end there and soon Dipa found herself drawn into an exchange on behalf of one of the workers who was having salary-related issues at work. While the case was settled in favour of the worker, Dipa realized how a little time and effort could make a big difference to someone's life — and in 2015 IRR was born. The initiative gradually snowballed into something much bigger and today has more than 1,200 volunteers on board.

Dipa looks up to Mahatma Gandhi, a lawyer like herself, for his imaginative and determined fight against the might of the British Empire. "He changed the tide completely," she says.

IRR has also tried to change public perception towards foreign workers who were somewhat maligned, especially after the Little India riots of 2013. It looks for innovative, imaginative and nimble ways to build bridges between Singaporeans and migrant workers.

Over the years, IRR has given out data cards for workers to phone home. Then there is the annual potluck meal where volunteers prepare the food and dine with the workers; among the treats are pizza, ice cream and roti prata, sponsored by eateries and individuals. Add to this a flea market, where pre-loved items such as clothes, electronics, water bottles and shoes are given away, free hair cuts can be had, and photo booths set up for the workers to take a snap or two and send home to family, making it a day of relaxation and fun for them.

In 2018, Dipa embarked on an ambitious plan to give each of the nearly 700,000 migrant workers in Singapore a Christmas present. She did not meet her target. Nonetheless, over 50,000 workers brought a gift home, thanks to the generosity of Singaporeans who opened their hearts to the noble idea.

IRR has also teamed up with several Starbucks outlets to collect unsold food that would otherwise be thrown away. Volunteers give out the food to migrant workers who they come across working on the roads or at construction sites.

IRR regularly requests Singaporeans to generously donate everyday utility items like tiger balm, toiletries, water bottles, backpacks and, not to forget, raincoats which started it all. The idea is to benefit the workers without taxing the donors.

Dipa helps workers irrespective of nationality. She has also helped the families of workers who have lost their jobs, been injured or died during the course of their work. She gives out her phone number freely and can be contacted over social media as well.

Walking the talk

Dipa grew up in Bangalore, India, in a progressive, well-educated family. She imbibed the virtues of caring for nature at an early age, feels strongly about the environment and is a passionate advocate of recycling. During her teens, she volunteered her time to teach children living in slums.

Her husband and children support her unconditionally. She says she is lucky to have a supportive spouse who steps up to take care of the children when she is busy. Her teenage sons often help her and she believes it is necessary to expose children from a young age to help others as kids have a natural lack of barriers. She was proved correct as during the pandemic, her older son started a student-led initiative to help migrant workers. The family took up Singapore citizenship in 2017.

"Open and forthcoming," is how Dipa describes herself. Not one to waste her time on idle pursuits, she does not like to be a mere spectator if she sees anything unfair. "If we can make a difference, we should speak up to make the world a better place," says Dipa, who is currently the Assistant General Counsel at a major telco.

When Covid-19 infections rose among migrant workers, IRR once again stepped up to distribute thousands of meals, essential items and hygiene products such as soaps, sanitizers and masks. Books, magazines and indoor games like carrom boards and playing cards were also sent to the dormitories to keep the workers occupied during quarantine.

Project Belanja, a brainchild of Senior Minister of State Ms Sim Ann, was another initiative supported by IRR. Thanks to various sponsors, partners and donors, more than 500,000 meals as well as biscuits, chips and coffee were provided to the workers.

Yet another IRR initiative is MAD Wish, which stands for 'Making a Difference While I Stay at Home'. Here migrant workers who are confined to their dormitories are given basic lessons in conversational English. The programme is available for workers who speak Bangla, Telugu, Thai and Burmese, and has been a resounding success.

Since March 2021, IRR has organized trips to the Singapore Flyer for migrant workers and they plan to bring many more on such rides. Online financial literacy classes are also being run jointly with DBS/POSB Bank. During vaccination drives at the dormitories, IRR partnered with the Ministry of Manpower by sending volunteers to assist the workers.

Teamwork makes dreams work

IRR has come a long way from being a one-person initiative to a body of volunteers, working towards strengthening the social fabric of Singapore. It is an organization with zero overheads, and with Dipa at its helm, espouses a cause that inspires and draws volunteers. During the pandemic, the entire IRR team went beyond the call of duty, working silently behind the scenes, without pay or compensation, to help the workers, says Dipa modestly.

Accolades are not new to Dipa. In 2016, she won the Sony IWA Woman of the Year Award and was featured in SingTel's 2016 National Day Campaign. In 2017, IRR was awarded the President's Award for Volunteerism & Philanthropy (Kampong Spirit). In August 2020, IRR was conferred the Shining World Compassion Award from the Supreme Master Ching Hai International Association. The year ended with Dipa being honoured with the President's Volunteerism & Philanthropy Award 2020 Special Edition in recognition of exemplary and selfless contribution towards care and compassion in Singapore.

Through social media, IRR has managed to draw attention and gain more publicity for their cause. On their Facebook and Instagram posts, they relay positive stories about migrant workers to raise the bar and encourage people to take a more definitive stance on their well-being. "During Covid-19, we have learnt lessons that we hope won't go to waste. So many groups have come forward to help the migrant workers," she explains.

Dipa's biggest reward is the joy of knowing that she has made Singapore more inclusive for migrant workers and given them a voice and a better future. This is a lady who has helped change untoward perceptions of foreign workers. They have a devoted champion in Dipa, who keeps her eyes and ears open to unfair practices and behaviours towards them.

"We have to put ourselves in the shoes of the less fortunate. Small acts of kindness make a big difference. We need to highlight the contributions of these unsung heroes," says Dipa passionately.

CROSS-CULTURAL INTERACTIONS THROUGH ART

"Artists are like sponges; they soak up everything from all cultures. Art sticks to us, we can borrow and absorb. Differences are stimulating. They engage me more than things that I have experienced before."

Milenko Prvacki

As one of Singapore's most prominent painters and art educators, Milenko Prvacki is a familiar name in the visual arts scene. The former Dean of Fine Arts at LASALLE College of the Arts first came to Singapore in 1991 and was involved in the construction of the now-defunct Maritime Museum. He held a couple of exhibitions at LASALLE and it was during this time that Brother Joseph McNally invited him to teach full-time at the college. Milenko's homeland Yugoslavia was crumbling due to civil unrest. Singapore, on the other hand, was gearing up for a thriving and buoyant arts scene.

"It was the beginning of my love for and dedication to Singapore," he recalls. "Brother McNally was an amazing man. He was not an artist but wanted to do something for the arts in Singapore." Milenko seized the chance and the rest, as they say, is history.

The visual dictionary that is Singapore

Milenko studied Fine Arts in Bucharest, Romania where he met and married his colleague Delia Prvacki, herself a well-known sculptor and artist. Before he moved to Singapore, Milenko was already an established name in Europe, having extensively exhibited there since 1971. As artists looking for peace and a suitable environment to get on with their crafts, Singapore seemed to be an oasis of calm and hope. At that time Singapore had only the National Museum catering to the arts, and the Singapore Symphony Orchestra for musical entertainment. The arts scene was being created from scratch. In Europe, it had been done and re-done many times over. For an artist, Singapore was an empty canvas and a tranquil space to practise one's craft.

The native Serbian speaker, who is also fluent in German and Romanian, faced his first challenge in Singapore when he had to learn another language — English. "When I moved here, I was always carrying a dictionary. I found it fascinating. It has so many words but no narrative. You can start reading it from anywhere. Through the dictionary it is possible to understand a language you don't know," says Milenko.

This is where he came up with the concept of a Visual Dictionary. Since he communicates through art, the Visual Dictionary is his language where he has mixed things that don't belong to each other, but all belong to one genre of visual arts — painting. Milenko has compiled all kinds of works together — figurative, geometrical, expressionist etc. — like words in a dictionary. Over the years, the prolific artist has created a profound body of work which has enriched the visual arts scene in Singapore.

He likens Singapore to a dictionary, where people of different nationalities, religions and languages live together in harmony to create a beautiful canvas of colours. To him, this racial harmony seems quite logical. The Yugoslavia of his childhood was also made up of different ethnicities and religions where everyone lived together peacefully. "We did not think it was odd or that we were different, and yet it all crumbled," he warns.

Milenko believes that there is no perfect place in the world, but Singapore is one of the best. He attributes Singapore's fast development to the government which has foresight and anticipates the needs of its citizens. Naturalized citizens like Milenko who come from different backgrounds can compare and appreciate what the government has done. "Many people call Singapore boring. But I enjoy boring. Moreover, it is well organized. As long as the system functions, I am fine," says Milenko who, along with his wife, took up Singapore citizenship in 2002.

Enriching the local arts scene

At LASALLE College of the Arts hundreds of students enrol annually, but only a few pick art as a vocation. Nonetheless, they are all taught to appreciate art. It's a handicap if people cannot enjoy art, feels the prolific artist who believes that art education should be introduced from an early age as it can help children communicate their thoughts and feelings.

In his early years, there weren't enough experienced art educators in Singapore. Milenko brought about a more professional and structured curriculum. A degree course was introduced, and he pioneered individual tutorials and group critique.

The group critique was a unique and revolutionary idea. Critique in an academic environment is especially important but students were upset as they were not used to people commenting critically on their work. Thanks to Milenko, it is now accepted as an important part of art education.

In 2005, Milenko started the Tropical Lab, an international art workshop that is held annually and is today a mainstay in Singapore's art calendar. Over two weeks, a well-chalked-out programme with seminars and international speakers culminates in an art exhibition. Artists and art students from around the world get an opportunity to present their work, giving local students exposure to international artists and an opportunity to experience different cultures and perspectives.

Milenko has served as Senior Fellow in the Office of the President at LASALLE since 2011. Most of Singapore's top artists today have been his students at some point or the other. He has exhibited extensively in Singapore and internationally and is well-known for his abstract works. In 2006, he was invited to exhibit at the Sydney Biennale and his works have found a place in the permanent collections of many museums worldwide.

He was part of the Renaissance City Strategic Plan Committee and the Marina Bay Advisory Committee set up to consider how the Singapore of the future would look like.

The art rehabilitation programme at Changi Prison has also benefitted from Milenko's involvement. Under his guidance, an art library was set up and space allocated for prisoners to create art while incarcerated. Over the years, a few inmates have enrolled at LASALLE after their release and have settled down to have families and regular jobs.

He has collaborated with his wife, a freelance ceramic artist, on several projects, the most notable and noticeable being the murals at the Dhoby Ghaut MRT station. The couple regularly engages in community art initiatives. They believe that since these events are free and easily accessible, they serve to educate people and everyone can enjoy them. That is also how the idea of the popular Art Week at Little India was born. Thanks to the patronage of the Singapore Tourism Board, it has become a regular event which is well-known for depicting the history of the area through wall art and installations.

Milenko is not afraid to speak his mind and believes that instead of repurposing heritage buildings, new venues should be created for displaying art with the aim of building for the future. "I am critical but not complaining. There is a difference. The only thing we should not comment on is religion and nationality because that is personal and must be respected. I am an active person in the arts scene but not an activist," says Milenko.

"Sometimes things grow too fast for their good and the same is the case with Singapore. There used to be a handful of artists, now there are thousands. There are so many theatres but not enough theatre groups. We are educating artists, building galleries, museums and cultural halls but not educating people sufficiently to appreciate them."

Milenko's artistic contributions have earned him several prestigious awards. He received the Cultural Medallion from the Singapore government in 2012, the first *ang moh* (Caucasian or white person) to receive it. The French government honoured him with the title of the Chevalier de l'Ordre des Arts et des Lettres (Knight of the Order of Arts and Letters). Ironically, in March 2020, he became the first non-Serb to receive the Sava Sumanovic Fine Art Award, the Serbian national award for visual arts. The former Serb says it was a nice feeling to receive it as a Singaporean.

Singapore is the place that he most identifies with now and claims he knows Singapore better than most Singaporeans. "Many Singaporeans haven't even seen Woodlands. They think it's some *ulu* (backward) place in the north, but that is where I have my lovely studio and where I live. I do my shopping at the Marsiling wet market, buying local stuff, and all the shopkeepers recognize me."

He may still be working on polishing his Singlish but the artist in him has well and truly found home.

SHAPING THE FUTURE OF BANKING

"The wealthy have already made it and the poorest sections of society receive help from the government and other agencies.
I worry about the lower middle class. They too need support, mentoring and a leg up to move up the curve."

Amit Sinha

Amit Sinha has a lot on his plate. He is Group Head of Telecom, Media & Technology within the Institutional Banking Group (IBG) at DBS, a role that he has filled for over a decade. The veteran banker has extensive experience and runs a truly regional franchise of a bank that has evolved into a leading Asian financial services company. But it wasn't always so, and banking came to Amit by accident.

Amit grew up in Nagpur, India, imbibing from his parents the solid middle-class virtues of hard work, dedication, focus and a drive to succeed. A gold medalist in Chemical Engineering from Nagpur University, he was comfortably working at a petrochemical plant when boredom and a desire to do something different changed the course of his career. The very small matter of not having enough funds to pay for his MBA programme at the Asian Institute of Management, Philippines did not deter Amit who took up summer internships, moonlighted as a part-time consultant and wrote reports for banks to see him through his two-year course. Amit not only graduated with a distinction, but this journey gave him an insight into finance and paved the way for a career in banking. It also brought to fore Amit's biggest strength — when he sets his mind to anything, he goes all out to achieve it.

Leading with focus and vision

The search for a perfect job that would satisfy the young man's growing aspirations brought him to Singapore. He didn't have to wait long and within a month he joined the Project Finance team at DBS. The year was 1999 and apart from a three-year stint in Dubai, Amit has been based in Singapore ever since.

DBS was at the cusp of transformation, gearing up to become a forward-looking bank. Amit's experience of living and working in India, Philippines, Dubai and Singapore helped him gain invaluable ground-level experience to understand the market, develop innovative solutions and connect with customers.

Twenty-two years later, he still tackles every task with his trademark enthusiasm. "I roll up my sleeves and get going. Unless you do it yourself you can't ask others to do it," states the man who loves his job which he says, "brings value not just to customers, but society as well."

In 2013, DBS opened its India desk with Amit at the helm. Amit supports the banking needs of Indian companies setting up offices outside India. He also had oversight of DBS's Middle East business at DBS Dubai for a period of seven years. But he has recently given up that role in the Middle East and started a new team, Platform Coverage, which helps start-ups raise funding in DBS's six core markets of China, India, Taiwan, Hong Kong, Indonesia and Singapore. The senior executive leads teams across Asia and in the process connects with customers across cultures. This ability to work in diverse geographies and plan a directionally correct route by creating a market strategy for the bank is a skill that Amit has acquired.

In 2018 Amit sponsored and spearheaded a data analytics project within IBG called 'Jellyfish' set up to assess risks, generate leads and find out possible opportunities for DBS to increase its business across various industry supply chains.

DBS has been at the forefront of digitalization in the banking sector and Amit is part of IBG's Digital Transformation Steering Committee which evaluates and brainstorms strategies and solutions to transform and digitize internal systems and processes, customer journeys and broader industry ecosystems. This is an important position, as the bank's digital strategy may hold the key to it maintaining its premier position among Asian banks.

Amit credits his success to being nimble and having the mindset and ability to drive through uncertainty, yet knowing clearly where to head and the confidence that he can make it work.

His external appointments include sitting on the Executive Committee of the South Asian Business group under the auspices of the Singapore Business Federation, to promote businesses in Southeast Asia. He represents DBS at the Singapore–India CEO Forum and actively promotes business between India and Singapore, linking both sides to work for mutual benefit. He is also part of the Singapore Indian Development Association's (SINDA) Indian Business-leaders' Roundtable, a non-profit organization comprising respected business leaders who not only contribute their expertise, networks and advice, but also work hand in hand with SINDA to uplift the Indian community in Singapore.

Amit humbly admits that he has had the good fortune to work with excellent bosses and colleagues who helped shape his career. Together they saw the right direction and created a market share for DBS, making it the premier bank in the region. He looks upon DBS Group CEO, Piyush Gupta, as inspirational and a role model who is focused on taking the bank forward in an increasingly digitized world.

The family man

Amit is a complete family man. His mother tongue Hindi is not forgotten and remains the lingua franca at home, keeping the family of four, comprising his wife and two kids, connected to their roots. Roots that taught Amit the virtue of integrity and nurtured in him a belief that no job is too trivial.

Amit tries to pass on his value system to his children. His daughter has worked part-time at a fast-food chain, and apart from it helping polish her Mandarin speaking skills — the second language that both she and her brother take at school — it has made her conscious of the financial difficulties faced by lower income families, school dropouts and the need for people to hold multiple jobs to supplement the family income. His wife volunteers with an organization that helps unwed mothers with their emotional, psychological and financial needs.

These interactions have led to interesting dinner table conversations and opened their children's eyes to the underbelly of Singapore, making them aware that behind the glitz there are people who could do with some help. Amit considers these as valuable lessons that will hold the children in good stead as they grow up to be conscious citizens of one of the world's most developed countries, of which they have been citizens since 2020.

His busy schedule notwithstanding, Amit makes time to volunteer as a member of the Management Committee at the Singapore Indian Fine Arts Society (SIFAS). "It's an opportunity for me to help SIFAS and the already bourgeoning Indian cultural environment to grow further," explains Amit who has been associated with SIFAS for many years. His daughter takes classes for Indian dance and his son is learning to play the tabla (drums) there.

He often ponders on the question of serving the society that has given him so much. The increasing divide between the haves and have-nots in the world bothers him. At work in DBS, he mentors youngsters but would now like to move outside his work sphere to help the youth in his personal capacity. He wants to impress on them the importance of education, help them develop confidence and encourage them to work towards their dreams.

Amit also sits on the advisory board of Billion Bricks, an organization that aims to build sustainable homes as a solution to homelessness. He uses his extensive experience and contacts to work out how the company can evolve in the future and remain a viable option.

Both professionally and personally Amit has felt welcomed in Singapore. He candidly admits that racial harmony, a meritocratic workplace with a level playing field and a well-nurtured society attracted him to Singapore.

He has made lifelong friends and sees himself growing old in Singapore, eating at his favourite hawker centre, and tossing *Lo Hei* on Chinese New Year for the continued prosperity and happiness of Singapore and Singaporeans.

MAKING THE IMPOSSIBLE POSSIBLE

"We should continue to have the spirit of adventure. There is no right or wrong, nor a perfect time. Just step out of your comfort zone and do it."

Khoo Swee Chiow

His is an inspiring story of pushing the boundaries of human endurance, of courage in face of tribulations, of perseverance and a relentless pursuit of dreams. Today, Khoo Swee Chiow dons the title of being the first Southeast Asian and fourth person in the world to complete the Adventure Grand Slam, having conquered the North Pole, the South Pole and the Seven Summits. He talks about his many achievements with his characteristic matter-of-fact charm.

The prolific mountaineer reads a lot and gets inspiration from famous climbers who went before him, like Tenzing Norgay and Edmund Hilary. He is a published author and motivational speaker who plans and leads adventure trips, gives mountaineering advice, and involves himself in charity and community works, all while dreaming up ideas for his next challenge.

The intrepid adventurer
Born in Port Dickson, Malaysia, Swee Chiow had a carefree childhood. Work brought him to Singapore in 1987. But for a fateful trip to the United States two years later where he tried his hand at mountaineering, life may have meandered on uneventfully for him. He was bitten by the sports bug, plunging headlong into it and trained intensively for three years. Climbing Mount Kilimanjaro in Tanzania fueled his appetite for more and that, coupled with grit and determination, led him to scale Mount Everest in 1998. It was the first-ever attempt by a Singaporean team to climb the highest mountain in the world.

Swee Chiow hasn't looked back since. He has climbed Everest three times, not a small achievement for a guy who was once afraid of heights. In 1999, Singapore's first homegrown professional adventure enthusiast went on a skiing trip to the South Pole. Next was an expedition to the North Pole, organized in collaboration with the Marine Parade Community Development Centre. Even though the trip wasn't successful — he had frostbite on his fingers and needed to be rescued — he still managed to raise $255,000 for intellectually disabled children and tetraplegics. His never-say-die attitude came to his rescue, and the very next year he successfully trekked the North Pole.

Swee Chiow went on to participate in the Riding for Life programme and along with other participants raised $50,000 for the NGO Action for Aids.

In January 2003, the SARS crisis hit Singapore. He felt the time was right to re-establish links with the country from where his forefathers had migrated. The idea was well-received by the Singapore–China Friendship Association. Swee Chiow pedalled 8,000 km through Malaysia, Thailand, Laos and Vietnam, before reaching Beijing.

In October 2007, he began a gruelling 94-day trip from Hanoi, Vietnam to Singapore — on inline skates! Covering a distance of some 6,000 km, he held press conferences along the way to draw attention to the importance of environmental conservation. "I wanted to tell the world that we don't need too much to live comfortably. If we are thrifty, we can still be happy and save the atmosphere," he says. A team of students from Shuqun Primary School accompanied him part of the way, for a hands-on experience in photojournalism, culture and geography.

In 2012 he climbed K2, universally considered the toughest and most dangerous mountain to climb. In 2019, after two failed attempts, he successfully scaled Mount Kanchenjunga, the world's third highest mountain. Every setback has made him more determined to live up to his philosophy: "You don't set out to fail. But if you dare not try, you have already failed."

His cycling skills came in handy once again when in June 2020, Swee Chiow pedalled around Singapore eight times — a distance of 1,088 km — to raise funds for the social initiative, It's Raining Raincoats. A total of $23,000 was raised and used to procure data cards and essential items for migrant workers.

Swee Chiow, who became Singaporean in 1999, confesses that he could accomplish many of his dreams because of his Singapore passport, which opens doors and smoothens the path considerably. The super-fit two-time Singapore Youth Award winner considers Singapore to be a land of opportunities, incredibly open and receptive to foreigners. He regularly volunteers his time with the National Youth Achievement Award Council, conducting motivational talks for the youth.

Dreaming big with eyes wide open

"Immigrants are hungry and determined to make it. They have nothing to lose," he quips. Climbing Mount Everest opened several avenues for Swee Chiow. His first-hand experience in organizing high-risk expeditions to surviving the most remote and hostile parts of the world came in handy when he quit his job in IT and turned his passion into a profession to become a full-time adventure tourism consultant.

"When I take people on expeditions, I have a heavy responsibility on my shoulders. Safety is my biggest concern; I know the routes, weather patterns and logistics. I have trusted Sherpas," he says candidly. Most of his clients are between 30 and 50 years old and mainly Singaporeans, but thanks to his name and fame, he also has clients coming from Thailand, Malaysia and Indonesia.

The adaptable and easy-going Swee Chiow has written five books about his adventures. He enjoys writing and telling stories. His journey is inspiring with the expected ups and downs. On more than one occasion, he has had to turn back due to unfavourable weather or lack of proper equipment, but he has never let it pull him down. "You are alive and that's all that matters. You can try again. Moreover, when you are down, you can only go forward," he says. This positivity has made him a much sought-after motivational speaker.

"Life teaches you a lot and I have turned my experiences into learnings and am using it to earn a living. My focus is on leadership and teamwork. Grab the opportunities that come your way, take some risks, plan well and through trial and error you will succeed. We are much stronger than we think." He adds, "People say Singapore has no mountains. I say we don't need mountains. We can still do it if we have the determination."

Among his biggest blessings is his family. He married his Singaporean wife, an adventure sports enthusiast herself, in 1996. They are parents to two teenagers, a son and a daughter. Ironically, his children hate climbing but share his love for the outdoors. His wife trusts his judgement implicitly, which makes Swee Chiow even more conscious of being safe for the sake of his family waiting for him to come home from one of his many adventures.

Singapore is a safe country, and this is what Swee Chiow feels has made Singaporeans risk averse. He is glad that the younger generation is more adventurous and open to climbing and extreme sports. "We need to learn to take well-calculated risks as competition is tough. We are efficient, smart and skillful but if we are not alert, others will overtake us. Many foreigners who come to Singapore cannot speak English, but they are so determined to succeed that they score As in their exams. Calculated risk-taking is therefore very essential," says Swee Chiow whose secret of success includes being adaptable, seizing the opportunity, being proactive and doing things well.

At 55, he still has a few mountains to climb. He dreams of sailing around the world, walking across a desert and doing things that have never been attempted before. The world is his oyster and Swee Chiow is already busy planning his next adventure.

CONTRIBUTING TO THE SINGAPORE STORY

"I am not here to change the system but to find the right tools to sustain myself in it and contribute positively."

Dr Bhanu Ranjan

She was a trailing wife who gave up a successful teaching career at a top university in India to follow her husband to Singapore when his job brought him here. Not just that, it also meant uprooting her children and leaving behind a settled, comfortable life to carve out a new path and rebuild her life in an unfamiliar country. Today, Dr Bhanu Ranjan feels that moving to Singapore was one of the best decisions she has made.

"People who come to this country do so because they see in Singapore something that they haven't seen elsewhere. They know the benefits of living here and once they are in Singapore, they put their best foot forward and give it their all. The government has done a wonderful job developing a superb infrastructure with a top-class education and healthcare system, and ensured a safe and conducive environment for its residents," explains Bhanu, who along with her family took up citizenship in 2014.

In her teens, Bhanu had wanted to serve in the Indian Air Force but had been dissuaded from doing so for various reasons. This dormant desire erupted in 2014 when the Singapore Armed Forces Volunteer Corps (SAFVC) was set up. The uniformed volunteer auxiliary encourages Singapore women, first-generation permanent residents and new citizens to undergo a basic military induction course and contribute towards national defence.

Bhanu did not think twice before registering and had to clear a medical test and pass an interview before she was accepted. At 40, she was among the oldest volunteers in her cohort. When asked by the interviewing officer why she wanted to serve, she countered with a "why not?". Bhanu has an interesting logic. "Everyone guards their house, it is the natural thing to do, and that's what I am doing." Her training at Pulau Tekong gave her a feel of the rigour that national servicemen have to go through. She is trained to use arms and should the need arise serve Singapore as part of a peacekeeping force.

This dynamic lady leads by example. By joining the armed forces, she did not just show a guiding path to her kids but became one of the thousands of Singaporeans who are equipped to protect Singapore in the event of an emergency.

Adapt, don't change

Bhanu, who has a PhD in Emotional Intelligence and Leadership Effectiveness, is currently an associate professor at the SP Jain School of Global Management. The opportunity to work with, and teach, a diverse cohort from various nationalities has given her a unique perspective and taught her to appreciate different people and cultures.

In the beginning, she admits being overwhelmed with the calibre of her colleagues and students. She quickly realized that Singapore attracts the best talent and knows how to nurture and sustain that talent. "Here you can't rest on your laurels because no one is irreplaceable," she says. "I am nervous every time I enter the class. And it is this nervousness that makes me give my best because in Singapore, nothing less than the best works."

She is putting her experience to good use by serving in her community centre and neighbourhood committee (NC). Currently, she is the Vice Chairman of the Integration and Naturalized Champions (INCs) at Mountbatten. This is a body of grassroots volunteers who help newcomers adapt, settle in and connect with fellow residents in the local community. She is also Vice Chairman at the Meyer NC and actively participates in blood donation drives, festive celebrations and other community events.

For Bhanu, community centres are an asset to every neighbourhood. They provide a common space for the residents to interact with one another while keeping their distinctive identities and cultural values.

Despite a busy professional schedule, she finds time to volunteer and always encourages more people to come forward and give back meaningfully to society. Her best reward is when residents appreciate her genuine desire to help and welcome her efforts.

Bhanu grew up surrounded by her mother and sisters, all of whom were strong women and a major influence on her, never letting her falter. From them she imbibed the indispensable virtues of humility, discipline and thrift, and picked up the art of 'scaffolding' — to help people move upwards.

Her family is her pillar of strength and conversations often revolve around her husband and two children. Her husband, a captain in the Merchant Navy, is her best critic. Her children have been her greatest teachers and Bhanu's window to the changing world. Her son, who is a keen debater, is currently doing his National Service. He studied at an international school, and never one to sit still, Bhanu actively met up with other expatriates to try to understand their culture and how they had made Singapore their home.

Integrating into Singapore as a family

Bhanu's experiences with the local community reinforced her resolve to send her daughter to a local school. "That was the only way we could channel her into the local culture. Moreover, local schools inculcate discipline," believes Bhanu.

Networking with parents from her children's schools, Bhanu realized that locals have quite a different perception of India. Many of them are unaware that India is so diverse and she shares her culture with them whenever the opportunity arises. Interacting with the parents also helped her understand Singapore and Singaporeans better.

An up-and-coming squash player, her daughter represented Singapore in the Swiss Open Under 13 Squash Championships in December 2019 and was ranked third. The family's heart swelled with pride when the diminutive teen climbed the podium and the flag of Singapore went up.

Bhanu does not have any role models per se. She appreciates anyone who is hardworking and humble, virtues she picked up from her father.

When faced with a problem, she will turn it into an opportunity to learn something new. In her own words, she is "creative crazy". If traffic is moving in one direction, she thinks about the possibility of moving in the opposite direction. It is not about rebelling, but about doing things differently with responsibility, accountability and commitment.

She says it's important to handle situations effectively without offending others. This is where her proficiency in negotiation and crisis management comes in handy. She recommends developing the right navigational tools to embrace differences tactfully.

Negotiation, to her, means understanding the other point of view, and is an essential skill to acquire in a multicultural society like Singapore. "If there is no clarity there will be confusion and misunderstanding so in any given situation, understanding the person and circumstances is the way forward."

She feels that Singaporeans are non-intrusive and quiet and would like them to open and communicate more. "It is important to feel the pulse and have the right awareness to channel thoughts in the right direction. In a social setting, it is equally important to let off steam to maintain equilibrium," she adds.

Bhanu, who wears many hats, is also a Transactional Analyst. She thinks deeply about how our actions help us transform into someone better. She regularly participates in workshops where discussions revolve around how and why things happen. It gives her a perspective and an awareness of issues and real-world requirements.

Her pride in her adopted home is evident. "I feel humbled when I think of the faith that the country and its people have reposed in me. It is a big responsibility. I need a safe country for my children and grandchildren. I chose this country, why would I not serve it?" she asks. "Singapore is like my plants, rooted yet growing. That is how I would like to live my life."

SERVICE WITH A SMILE

"God opened doors for me, and I came to Singapore. Singapore received me with open arms and for that I am grateful."

Chew Ai Mei

"See what you can do for Singapore, not what Singapore can do for you," says Chew Ai Mei, an active grassroots leader at the West Coast Park Neighbourhood Committee (NC). NCs are the equivalent of a Resident's Committee for those living in private estates and were established in 1998 to encourage residents to be more active and strengthen community bonds.

In the last five years, Ai Mei has helped organize a variety of major events in her NC, including Earth Hour and Project Sunshine, as well as tree planting activities. She was the initiator and organizing chairman for the Mooncake Festival and the National Day NC event in 2017 and 2018 respectively.

Also in 2017, she took up the position of chairlady of the managing committee in her condominium. As it was a new estate, she had to put in place proper procedures and practices and ensure that things ran smoothly. There were many teething problems, but she managed to overcome them and win over the residents with her years of experience and positive attitude.

Moving to the next milestone

Ai Mei was born in Johor Bahru but grew up in Petaling Jaya, Malaysia. She moved to Singapore in the year 2000, after being headhunted for the position of sales director for Asia-Pacific at a software company. Since young, it had been her dream to live in Singapore. Her family often visited the city-state, and she was always fascinated by the clean city and efficiency that she experienced here.

Her early days in Singapore were fraught with difficulties, but intent on achieving her goals, she overcame any obstacles through determination, perseverance and a positive mindset.

Her role model has always been the former late Prime Minister Lee Kuan Yew, whom she looks up to for his integrity of character and honest governance. She particularly appreciates that Singapore values its citizens and focuses on their welfare without discriminating on grounds of race, language or religion.

It was not too difficult for Ai Mei to adjust to life in Singapore as Malaysia is also multiracial, with similarities in food and culture. Ai Mei speaks English, Malay and Cantonese, which she says helps her connect with a large cross-section of people. Through her marriage, becoming a mother and reaching new career heights in Singapore, she has never once forgotten to be grateful for all the comforts that Singapore has offered her.

With her passion for the Lion City, it was a no-brainer that she took up citizenship in 2015 and started to look for ways to give back to the country. On National Day the following year, she chanced upon an event held in her housing estate and asked the event organizer at the NC how she could help. That was the start of her journey in volunteering. One of the first people she met was the NC's then chairperson, Mr. Prakash Hetamsaria, whom she regards highly for the camaraderie he built with other NC members to foster togetherness and belonging among locals and new immigrants.

"There are so many people doing so much good work that I feel very small compared to them," says the humble but ever-smiling Ai Mei.

Sowing the seeds of community bonding

Ai Mei is clear that grassroots work is not for those who think of it as a pastime or an opportunity to take photographs with ministers. It's a lot of hard work as every event must be planned well and to the minutest detail if it is to be successful. Volunteers must be willing to contribute their personal time and energy.

"I am an honest, hardworking, determined person and I'm always up-to-date with technology. In that sense, I am just like Singapore," she adds. Not one to sit on her laurels, Ai Mei has taken several courses over the years to enhance her skills and keep up with the latest developments, and has completed the Professional Certification in Digital Marketing programme from the Singapore Management University. She is currently a digital marketing trainer and financial analyst.

Ai Mei, who also holds a master's degree in Business Administration from the University of South Australia, is using her knowledge and experience to contribute to the community. She has seen the impact of technology and a changing job market on job security. With more people being retrenched, she gives talks to encourage those who have been displaced to upgrade or learn new skills and not feel redundant, and to look out for appropriate job opportunities. She has also conducted several training programmes for professionals, managers, executives and technicians (PMETs) on employability, financial management and entrepreneurship.

Ai Mei trains senior citizens to be digitally ready so that they are not left out in an increasingly digitized world. She wants to help them to be comfortable engaging with technology and acquaints them with the various e-banking and e-commerce apps. Her friendly and approachable demeanour makes her immensely popular with the elderly and there is always a request for her to conduct more classes.

She is actively involved in the SG100 Foundation, a "social enterprise established with the purpose of building a strong foundation to establish a prosperous and sustainable future for Singapore." As a mother of an 18-year-old, she strongly feels that it is the youth who need to be mentored, as they will be the leaders of tomorrow. "Even if I just lend a listening ear to the youth, I will feel I have achieved something," says the lady whose husband is quietly supportive and proud of all that his wife does.

In 2020, as the world entered a crisis caused by the Covid-19 pandemic, Ai Mei did not just sit back and watch from the safety of her home. She helped to distribute masks to the community and volunteered at the Crisis Relief Alliance (CRA), a non-profit organization that supports communities in crisis. As a volunteer manager, she helped recruit, manage and organize the volunteers who would distribute fruits, snacks, beverages and other essentials to migrant workers in the dormitories.

Her spirit of service, drive to volunteer and desire to give back to society come from within and from her faith, says Ai Mei. This, she says, is what she wants to focus on as it enables her to make a difference in other people's lives in the community.

Ai Mei herself has benefitted from serving society. Volunteering has helped push her out of her comfort zone and improved her problem solving abilities. It has enabled her to learn new skills, meet people from different walks of life and gain valuable experiences.

Her message for all new Singaporeans: "Run with the vision of Singapore, otherwise, you will be left behind. More importantly have a charitable heart towards the community and your new home."

THE ART,
THE ARTIST,
AND HIS VISION

"I dream a lot. Dreams activate the mind. I don't forget my dreams. I observe these influences that have been bestowed on me by nature. They keep my mind childlike and innocent."

Rosihan Dahim

Rosihan Dahim has been a prominent figure in the Singapore art scene for over four decades. He is undoubtedly one of the pioneers of the Surrealist art form in Singapore, a painting technique that allows the unconscious mind to express itself freely. His work covers a wide range of themes: dreams, psychology, history, climate change, world peace and philosophy.

Yet, for all his fame, there is a childlike simplicity that makes it possible for him to see things in a manner that eludes most adults. His work may confuse the casual observer, but has a deeper purpose when seen through his eyes. It underlines a continuous and indefinable search for knowledge and understanding. There is introspection for what could have been, and an awareness of the need to be more humane and tolerant in the future.

The making of an artist

Born in Singapore in 1955 to Indonesian parents, Rosihan divided his time between Singapore and his grandmother's home in Java, Indonesia. During the Second World War, his father fought along with the HMS British Navy and was interred in Singapore as a prisoner of war when his battleship was sunk. He would often share his experiences with Rosihan, which left a deep impression on the young boy. By the time he was in primary school, Rosihan had started doodling and was often pulled up for not focusing on his studies.

The makings of a future artist could be seen clearly, when at the age of 13 he won the third prize for art at the Singapore Youth Festival. Ironically, he went on to fail an art exam in secondary school. The teacher asked the class to draw a picture of a thief stealing an umbrella from an old lady, but he drew an old lady hitting the thief with her umbrella. "For me that was logical," says Rosihan. "That's how I saw the scene in my mind's eye."

Rosihan continues to defy boundaries and create works that depict his perception of things, and not how other people see them.

The avid reader of books on human behaviour and the paranormal pursued his education at the Nanyang Academy of Fine Arts, where he was strongly influenced by Dadaism and the works of Surrealist European artists of the 1920s. According to him, his works are "visually thought-provoking and questioning"; they follow in the tradition of Surrealist artists but also display the influence of his Indonesian roots.

He demonstrates his creativity through the medium of oil, acrylic, watercolour, pencil, ink, sculpture and assemblage art. His works are rendered in brilliant colours but are at times monochromatic.

In the early years, some critics found his works strange. However, many soon conceded that what makes his art timeless and relevant is that he sees things in the subconscious and beyond the conscious mind. Rosihan is quick to admit that the same painting may be perceived by two people in different ways. Through his work, he challenges preconceptions about art. "We have been given two lives, one real and the other imaginary," he says. For Rosihan, his art is a visual reflection of the inner workings of his mind. In 2014, the surrealist artist published the book *One Mind One Theory*.

An iconic feature of his art is the matchstick, which he employs to depict the human mind. It harks back to a childhood memory of his father collecting matchsticks in a jar. Though tiny in real life, the matchstick adds another dimension to Rosihan's art. One of his earliest works, *Escapade* (1978), portrays him with his two siblings as matchstick figures.

His first solo exhibition at the National Museum Art Gallery in 1980 won him instant recognition. It introduced Singapore to surrealism and made people sit up and notice Rosihan and his work. In 2010, he painted the 12 mythical animals of the Chinese zodiac. Superimposing these with a red dot, Rosihan, who has an amazing eye for detail, represented Singapore's journey and its sustenance through difficult times via the characteristic strength of each animal.

The multitalented artist has created sculptures for environment design and architecture and many hotel projects. One of his commissioned works depicts a bird's eye view of Singapore, which he says makes him joyful and proud of his homeland.

His works have been featured on magazine covers, documentaries and publications, and are part of collections in Asia, Europe and the USA. He regularly participates in international exhibitions and art symposiums, and has several awards to his name, notably the Australian Art Award (1985), Philip Morris Art Award (1995 and 1996) and Ocean Artist of The Year Award (2010).

To commemorate the bicentenary of Sir Stamford Raffles' arrival in Singapore in 1819, a 270-metre-long painting depicting the nation's past, present and future was displayed at the Chingay Parade in 2019. Rosihan was one of three artists involved in creating this unique piece. As he took on the responsibility of creating the storyboard, he read and researched extensively to choose the most iconic images that best represent the city-state. To visualize the future dreams and aspirations of Singaporeans, Rosihan delved into his imagination and came up with a drawing in which Singapore was enclosed within an air-conditioned dome-like structure with a lot of greenery to protect it from global warming. A stingray shaped aircraft — a futuristic airline — floated above. Rosihan, who enjoyed working with the other artists, feels that "in real life, we should not create unnecessary boundaries that may lead to conflict."

Dreams and the subconscious mind

There have been times when Rosihan's identity as a Singaporean was questioned. "People see my name and ask me where I am from. My art seems foreign to them too. But my passport marks me as Singaporean. The Indonesian flag is red and white. Add Singapore's crescent moon and stars to it, and that is me. I have the advantage of having the influences of both countries enrich my life. Becoming Singaporean was a choice that has completed my journey," says the artist, who took up citizenship in 1976 and represented Singapore at the Venice Biennale in 2017.

He believes that the human brain has a vast amount of capacity and is capable of doing much. Unlike a robot, it can delve deeper and look beyond what is visible. He compares his mind to a thumb drive that captures and preserves all that he sees around him. He does not erase or delete the information but saves it, drawing on it when required.

In Singapore, he feels valued as he has received widespread appreciation and respect for his works. He is a big fan of Singapore's first prime minister Lee Kuan Yew for his ability to enhance the growth of Singapore and nurture it to what it is today.

Rosihan has worked with and taught art to the hearing impaired. The experience has given him an appreciation of the differences among people in the world. He has been part of the Elephant Parade to raise funds for charitable causes, and has auctioned his artwork to support organizations like the Animal Concerns Research and Education Society, the Singapore General Hospital Needy Patients Fund and the Singapore Cancer Society.

"Singapore is my land. I took up citizenship once I turned 21. It was a conscious decision. We humans belong to the same earth and share the same world. How we resolve our views, absorb influences and figure out the unknown depends on us. We have to understand what we are and the reason why we have been created. We must look beyond race, religion or colour. Religion is for our guidance, a way to live our lives. God did not create borders. He created one earth and one family in humanity," explains the artist whose faceless matchstick figures represent this belief.

Rosihan feels blessed to be able to imagine the unknown and use it to put not just Singapore but Southeast Asia on the world map of Surrealist art.

NURTURING OUR YOUTH THROUGH SPORTS

"Singapore is a land of opportunity. It spoils you. To make it your own you have to integrate, be a real person with real emotions. That's the only way forward."

Aleksandar Duric

Aleksandar Duric counts receiving his Singapore citizenship in 2007 as one of the proudest moments of his life. He had come to Singapore on his own accord, not on a government-backed initiative. Being a citizen allowed him to play football for Singapore. Then 37 years old, an age when athletes have long hung up their boots, Aleksandar went on to score 27 goals in 54 games for Singapore and a total of 387 goals in domestic matches. He also became Singapore's first foreign-born football captain.

Striving for the best

Aleksandar first came to Singapore in 1999 to play for Tanjong Pagar United. The next year he donned the jersey of Home United, subsequently playing for Geylang United, the Singapore Armed Forces and Tampines Rovers. At the age of 42, he became the oldest player to score in the Suzuki Cup, a regional football competition. His eyes light up when he recalls the glory of playing at the old National Stadium and Jalan Besar Stadium in front of a cheering home audience, united as one nation, focused on raising the Singapore flag to victory. In 2011, the International Federation of Football History and Statistics hailed him as one of the most prolific goal scorers in the world. However, it is not the number of goals but the honour of being able to play for Singapore that fills him with gratitude.

Aleksandar credits his success to a disciplined lifestyle and hard work, values that are inherent in Singapore's work culture as well. The former kayaker who, at one time, had served in the Yugoslav army, is a strong supporter of National Service and believes that "a stint in the army turns boys into men".

Aleksandar's youth was scarred by a brutal civil war that forced him to leave Yugoslavia, the country of his birth. His father and brother fought in the war; his mother, tragically, died from a bombing. In his autobiography *Beyond Boundaries*, Aleksandar details the difficult circumstances he faced while being separated from his family for over a decade. Sports became Aleksandar's refuge from personal tragedy and the reason for his future triumph when he was chosen as one of the first to represent Bosnia in the Olympic Games in kayaking.

In 2014, Aleksandar retired from playing professional football. Since 2016, he has served as the Principal of the ActiveSG Football Academy. He has nearly 3,000 youths under his wing and hopes some of them will play professionally in the future or at least develop a lifelong love for sports, because sports fosters camaraderie, a spirit of fair play, resilience and sportsmanship — all qualities essential in future citizens.

"I want our sports scene to be better and stronger. Someone must open their mouth and I am willing to play the devil's advocate, if that gives kids the chance to have better facilities and opportunities. If the system fails, I take the blame as I am a part of the system," says Aleksander. Honest to the point of being blunt, he does not believe in mincing his words when it comes to sports.

Forging familial bonds

For many years, Aleksandar was a nomad travelling from country to country until he found peace of mind and a family in Singapore. Singapore became his forever home and he lives in an HDB flat in Holland Village. He has four children, two of whom are adopted.

The former Chairman of Tampines Rovers, Teo Hock Seng, has been a father figure and role model to Aleksandar. "He showed faith in my ability as a player. His family became my family," says an emotional Aleksandar who is immensely grateful for his guidance and support. Aleksandar validated the faith reposed

in him manifold by leading Tampines Rovers to a hat-trick of
S-League titles.

He counts people of all races as his friends and enjoys
learning about their value system and religious beliefs, coming
out richer as a person through the process. "Foreigners must
remember this is not their country. For the privilege of being
allowed to be here, they should respect the culture, work along
with locals and adapt. They should not hide in their expensive
condominiums, but come out and mix with the heartlanders,"
says Aleksandar, who is Serbian by ethnicity.

The old Chinese lady down the corridor from his flat
occasionally brings him food. People in the street recognize
him and come up to shake hands. Cab drivers are thrilled to
be ferrying a celebrity in their car, almost always striking up
conversations about football, leading his kids to roll their eyes
because they must listen to "daddy stories". "I didn't realize that
people cared," he says with a twinkle in his eyes. "It means so
much to me because it shows they have accepted me as one
of them."

Today, he has enough for his needs, but things were not
always so, and Aleksandar is conscious that there are people
around who could do with some help. He loves working with
children. On why he has adopted two children along with
having a son and a daughter of his own, he explains: "Our future
is in the kids. They need our love and guidance. When and if
I have more money, I would love to provide a home to more."
Aleksandar has run a marathon to raise funds for a children's
home. Once, he even chauffeured passengers and donated the
money raised to The Straits Times School Pocket Money Fund.

As a council member of the Singapore Kindness Movement
(SKM), he feels that "Singaporeans in particular and Asians in

general don't express their emotions much. Even when we have to express gratitude we find it difficult to do so. An organization like SKM serves as a reminder that we should do kind deeds daily because it benefits both the person and the community."

In 2015, he was appointed as the first ambassador of the Delta League by the National Crime Prevention Council (NCPC). The Delta League is a youth outreach and engagement programme jointly organized by the Singapore Police Force and the NCPC to keep youth meaningfully occupied during school holidays and raise their awareness about crime prevention.

He places a lot of emphasis on the role sports play in our lives and is of the strong opinion that sports can bring a nation together. "Our lives have been taken over by technology. Playing games is essential for the good health of the body, the mind and the soul too. All you need is one ball to get people of different religions and races to come together to play, grow, bond and build social skills," says Aleksandar.

He speaks from experience when he says, "with the growing lack of tolerance and respect for the beliefs of others, now more than ever, we must remind our children to be open-minded. When I was growing up, ethnicities and religion never crossed our minds, yet my country was embroiled in a horrific civil war. People should not become selfish and self-centred. It must be drilled into the younger generation that this is their home."

Aleksandar has nothing but gratitude for being given the opportunity to serve his adoptive country. "It is not my pink identity card that makes me Singaporean; it is my total integration in the food, culture and language that makes me one. I barely spoke any English when I first came. It is here that I learnt English so Singlish comes naturally to me." His friends often refer to him as "the guy with an *ang moh* body and a Singaporean soul".

Nothing has come easily to Aleksandar. He has lived a life under tremendous pressure but believes that pressure brings out the best in him. He has worked hard and made sacrifices to reach his position. For him, hunger for success and not succumbing to anything dishonourable is what true sportsmanship is all about.

There is immense thankfulness in everything he utters and his love for Singapore is apparent. "The Merdeka generation has worked hard to bring the country where it is. For us naturalized citizens, we can only give and be grateful for the opportunity to call the Little Red Dot home. I could have been anywhere in the world, but I came here because somewhere in the unknown past, I was connected to this place. It was my destination and my destiny."

LEARN, ADAPT AND PRACTISE: THE MANTRA FOR SUCCESS

"I have carried the flag of Singapore at several international radiology-related events. It is an immense responsibility as well as an honour. The whole world looks upon Singapore's representatives to be one of the best, so the pressure is immense."

Cornelio Gutierrez Padre

Arriving in Singapore for what he thought would be a short stint as a radiographer, Cornelio Gutierrez Padre was struck by the state-of-the-art medical equipment and opportunities afforded to him here. Two decades later Cornelio — fondly called Nhel — still works for his first employer, the Singapore General Hospital (SGH).

Cornelio, who moved here from the Philippines and became a Singapore citizen in 2009, brought with him extensive professional experience from his home country. Yet, he was taken by surprise at the advanced state of medical technology available to health professionals and how common it was to use expensive procedures to make a better and more accurate diagnosis. Always ready to broaden his horizons, Cornelio quickly embraced the opportunity to learn and operate advanced medical equipment and assist doctors when required.

Having a learning mindset

"SGH is very supportive when it comes to career enhancement and invests in grooming professionals, giving the right persons the right exposure and augmenting their qualification according to their ability for mutual benefit," explains Cornelio, who is currently a principal radiographer at SGH.

He has been given opportunities to go for advanced training in hospital management, and has attended development programmes and online courses — all sponsored by his company. He has assiduously furthered his techniques and knowledge by participating in various local, regional and international conferences.

In fact, he is one of the pioneer radiographers to use Computed Tomography Angiography. Since 2008, he has been operating a Hybrid CT Angiography system and has contributed to the development and improvement of Intra-arterial CT Angiography protocols and imaging clinical applications in Interventional Radiology.

In the fast-evolving field of medical technology, there are constant challenges and Cornelio tackles them head-on. He also organizes events where best practices in his sphere of work are shared and trains newcomers, including professionals from other hospitals in Singapore.

He was lucky because Singapore was one of the first countries in Asia outside Japan to acquire state-of-the-art CT Angiography equipment, and other countries were looking towards Singapore to learn more about it. He feels privileged to have been chosen to present his research at conferences in Philippines, Australia, Thailand, Japan and many other countries.

It was not easy. "At an event like the International Society of Radiographers or the Radiological Technologists World Congress where thousands of top-notch radiographers from all over the world are present, I have to present something unique and local. I am representing not just myself or SGH, but Singapore," says Cornelio.

Small acts of kindness make a big difference

Cornelio has not forgotten his early days in Singapore when he was alone and looking for like-minded friends. This was when he turned to his church and joined their choir group. Within a few years, swayed by the cleanliness, peace and order that are a hallmark of Singapore society, he was convinced that his future lay in Singapore and he brought his wife and two daughters here. Incidentally, both daughters are healthcare professionals in Singapore.

For the last several years, Cornelio has been President of the Association of Filipino Radiographers in Singapore (AFRIS). It was founded in 2010 to promote camaraderie and foster harmonious relationships among the radiographers and their colleagues. From his own experience, he is well aware of the difficulties young Filipino radiographers may face as they try to settle into the work culture in Singapore. He believes that radiographers, though a part of the healthcare community, are less known. But like other health professionals, they also suffer from occupational stresses and burnouts. Keeping this in mind AFRIS tries to create a support system to help them cope and increase their stress tolerance while disseminating information on professional advancement opportunities.

There have been occasions when Cornelio has had to step in to help sort out issues before they became too big, by providing a listening ear in a confidential and non-judgemental manner. The association organizes activities for its members, such as inter-hospital basketball games, to keep them in high spirits and develop camaraderie amongst them.

AFRIS organizes humanitarian activities as well. In collaboration with the Philippine embassy in Singapore, members visit Filipino domestic helpers in distress, providing them with food, gifts and lend a listening ear to them. They volunteer at Willing Hearts, a non-affiliated charity which operates a soup kitchen for the elderly, disabled and needy. The AFRIS officers have also initiated and organized fundraisers to aid victims of natural disasters in the Philippines.

Not forgetting his birth country, in 2013, Cornelio co-founded Tambayang Adorable in San Leonardo Nueva Ecija, a non-partisan group which gives out Christmas presents to hundreds of Filipino children during the festive season.

If there is one person whom Cornelio is grateful to, it is Professor Tan Bien Soo who recognized his abilities and gave him professional support early on. Prof Tan, who is now a Senior Consultant with the Department of Vascular and Intervention Radiology and Chairman, Division of Radiological Sciences at SGH, "challenged, supported, recognized and appreciated" his talents and without his encouragement, Cornelio believes he would never be where he is today.

"Moreover, the Radiology Department at SGH is like a family," he adds. "Everyone is helpful and adjusting. Despite being a naturalized citizen, I never felt discriminated against and was given every opportunity to further my interests." Undoubtedly, Cornelio himself had the right ethos, qualities and attributes necessary for success.

He cherishes the memory of meeting the then Minister of Health, Khaw Boon Wan, at an official dinner. "I had been here only for a few years and it was so nice of him to have asked me how I was and if I was doing well." It is incidents like these that remind him that making Singapore his home was the right decision.

In 2020, faced with the Covid-19 crisis, healthcare workers were the most affected and busier than ever. Along with his regular job, Cornelio had to juggle additional responsibilities, such as reviewing the work schedules in his department to maintain social distancing while ensuring that work could continue. "That is one thing about Singapore; it does not sit back and relax but learns from every experience and doesn't repeat its mistakes," says Cornelio whose experience during the time of SARS came in handy.

Cornelio has adapted to Singapore, thanks to the well-organized system of governance. He is not worried when his daughters venture out for work or relaxation at odd hours due to the safe social environment. Moreover, he finds Singaporeans, like Filipinos, are very family oriented.

If there is one thing that he has learnt from living in Singapore, it is discipline. For Cornelio, it is the secret behind Singapore's success and a quality worth emulating.

Singapore has been good for Cornelio. "When you come to Singapore, follow the law and be disciplined. Do not bring bad habits here. Be a part of the Singapore story; embrace challenges that every advanced country has. You cannot cope or survive if your mind is inflexible. The more you try the farther you get," says Cornelio, who has made a life for himself in Singapore by living by these principles.

THE LANGOLI
LAO SHI

"Through tradition, bonding, and in promoting my own culture, I have connected with other races. It is particularly important to be aware of one's tradition and culture, and at the same time learn about and appreciate other cultures as well."

Vijayalakshmi Mohan

At an age when people complain of painful knees and are happy to retire and play with their grandchildren, Vijayalakshmi Mohan is busy making an international name for herself as a professional rangoli artist.

Sitting on her haunches, the talented grandmother of two creates unique rangolis for hours. Vijaya, as she is popularly known, has single-handedly put Singapore on the world rangoli map, having represented the island nation in showcasing this traditional Indian floor art form all over the world.

The roots of her love for rangoli go back to a time when as a little girl growing up in Trichy, India, she started making rangolis after watching her mother create them on the floor of their home every morning. She would also walk around the neighbourhood and copy all the fascinating rangoli designs she came across in a notebook. Fifty years on, the self-taught artist holds the Guinness World Record for the largest rangoli ever created (awarded in 2003) and has 32 other Singapore records in various categories under her belt.

Vijaya moved to Singapore in 1992 and loves everything about it. "This country saw my potential, appreciated my talent, encouraged me, and gave me opportunities and avenues to showcase it," reflects Vijaya, who became a citizen in 2005.

Making traditional art contemporary

Vijaya has cast a spotlight on rangoli art that has hitherto been limited to Indian homes and courtyards.

One of the early ways she applied her expertise was when a leading hotel in Singapore approached her to make a rangoli on a carpeted floor. The talented Vijaya came up with a new idea and Singarangoli, a Singapore version of the traditional rangoli, was born. Instead of limiting herself to traditional white rice or colourful rangoli powders, she incorporated a variety of materials in her work, such as galvanized iron sheets, broken bangles, pasta, sago and cotton buds.

In her extensive use of unique materials and methods, the internationally acclaimed artist sees a reflection of Singapore's multicultural society, where people of different races come together to form a beautiful whole.

Keeping in mind Singapore's unpredictable weather, she made her first all-weather rangoli at the Esplanade. It involved over 950 people who teamed together to create the world's first outdoor rangoli on the occasion of Indian Arts Festival Kalaa Utsavam. A special glue was used to help the materials stay in place for almost two months. In 2016, Vijaya was invited to display her art at a medical centre in the US state of Nebraska. She decided to go eco-friendly and used only materials that were easily accessible like recycled CDs, sawdust, and plastic spoons and forks.

Under her expert hands, the rangoli has evolved and adapted to modern times, moving from floor to table, to the wall and the ceiling. She has even made rangoli on water and underwater. The artist in her works tirelessly, planning new designs, preparing the materials, and testing them under different conditions so as to keep this traditional art form alive. "Just like Singapore, my rangolis are constantly evolving to stay relevant to the times, otherwise they will be out of place in modern society and die like many other traditional arts," says the renowned artist.

Art as therapy

A lifelong learner with a constant thirst for self-improvement and knowledge, Vijaya has earned for herself a certificate in Preschool Management and Administration and a diploma in Special

Education from the National Institute of Education, as well as a master's in Art Therapy from the LASALLE College of the Arts.

This former special education teacher and art therapist is a strong believer in the power of colours, which she uses not just to express herself but also to connect with society. In 2018, she visited the Singapore General Hospital and demonstrated her passion to the patients, nurses, junior doctors and visitors. Under her guidance, some 450 rangolis were created and exhibited on the walls of the hospital.

"Colours," she says, "provide strong sensory stimulation to uplift moods and improve behaviour. They give physical and emotional energy to participants which in turn leads to improved self-confidence and esteem."

She is also the creator of the Rangoli Puzzle Dazzle where rangolis are made in the form of colourful and eye-catching jigsaw puzzles. The individual pieces stand for the struggles of patients and bringing the pieces together represent the journey of patients towards recovery and better health. Vijaya believes that working on these puzzles serves the dual purpose of entertaining as well as stimulating the brain.

Her healing art activities have been successfully conducted at several places including the Jamiyah Nursing Home, AWWA Senior Activity Centre, Dementia Care Centre for Seniors, St Andrew's Nursing Home and Dover Park Hospice.

Not shy to promote herself and her art for the greater good of the community, Vijaya volunteers at schools, old age homes, hospitals, community centres and other medical facilities. The elderly residents who she volunteers her time with, often call her 'Langoli *Lao Shi*' or rangoli teacher in Mandarin.

She runs the Pure Hearts Recreation Centre, which is open to people of special needs and of all races and age groups. The centre organizes activities held at various community centres where attendees pick up recreational skills like drawing, dancing and playing the drums. Vijaya is always present at these events and over the years many have come to call her 'Amma' or mother. Her students, she says with evident pride, regularly participate in the Chingay Parade.

She works with several voluntary welfare organizations that recognize her talent and appreciate how her programmes benefit their members. In 2018, the Whampoa Community Centre gave her the Long Time Community Service Award for 15 years of service.

During the Covid-19 pandemic, she gave clapping hands therapy workouts thrice a week to patients at the Institute of Mental Health and once a week to the elderly residents at Sree Narayana Mission.

Vijaya continues to conduct training and consultancy workshops in rangoli making and art therapy.

Social harmony through art

Her rangolis often reflect racial harmony. Multicultural symbols like dragons, hong baos, ketupats, Malay daggers, bells and flowers have all been a part of her rangoli designs at some point. In a fusion of Chinese and Indian culture, around 30 voluntary welfare organizations teamed up with Vijaya in 2017, to create a display of art and lantern pieces at Gardens by the Bay.

To commemorate Singapore's bicentennial in 2019, Vijaya was invited to work with two other local artists to create an art piece titled "Our Past, Present and Future". The trio worked under trying weather conditions to complete the 270-metre-long painting, which was used as the centerpiece for the Chingay Parade. The same year, she guided students at an international school to create a vibrant orchid — the Vanda Miss Joaquim, Singapore's national flower — with toothpicks.

Living in multiracial Singapore has taught her to adapt and adjust. A staunch vegetarian, Vijaya in her growing up years was not used to meat being served at her table. "I am more tolerant today, especially because I see how much effort people take to arrange vegetarian food for me," she explains.

Her humility belies her fame. In spite of her numerous awards and packed schedule, she does not sit back and rest on her laurels. She learnt to work on computers when she was in her late forties and is currently toying with the idea of doing a doctoral degree and writing a book.

Her giving spirit has taught her children and grandchildren to reach out to the community in different ways. Her young grandsons observe their *patti* (grandmother) eagerly. "Rangoli and all the colours that go with it make me ecstatic. I am learning from her and one day we will together make a world record," says her eight-year-old grandson who is ready to take her legacy forward.

Vijaya believes that immigrants can integrate better if they come with a sense of belonging, and not forget to give back to society by volunteering their time and talent. "Wherever we live we should strive to be comfortable and make the people around us also at ease. We cannot just take, we must learn to live holistically by sharing our knowledge, experience and culture."

Happiness in what she does fuels Vijaya. After bending over a rangoli for long hours, there are times when she thinks of taking a break, but the smiles that her artwork brings to people's faces keeps her going. "I believe in *Manav Sewa* — service to humanity and through them I serve God."

EMBRACING THE CORE SINGAPORE VALUE OF COHESIVENESS

"Because we like this place, because we felt deeply for Singapore, we chose to work, learn, reside, sink our roots and raise our family here. It was a difficult decision, but we made our choice – Singapore is our new home."

Tony Du Zhiqiang

His first job in Singapore was as the manager of a poultry factory. It was 1991. Tony Du Zhiqiang single-handedly set about mechanizing the newly established production unit. His humility, sincerity and diligence put him in good stead as he did not shy away from learning and doing even the most basic of jobs. Like most immigrants, the mechanical engineer had the drive and work ethic to succeed and within one year, his company posted an annual profit of more than two million dollars. This training ground effectively put Tony on the road to success.

Having grown up in Chengdu, in the Sichuan province of China, Tony is no stranger to hard work. He graduated from Southwest University of Science and Technology in Sichuan with a bachelor's degree in mechanical engineering. He was among the first batch of students who entered university after China resumed college entrance exams in the 1970s.

During a business trip to Singapore in 1988, he was impressed by the bourgeoning city-state and recognized that there was ample scope for well-qualified professionals like him to make a mark. Seizing the opportunity, Tony moved to Singapore in 1991.

This was a time when Singapore was at the cusp of becoming a global technology and financial hub. There was a need for skilled workers to work in places like factories and shipyards. While working at the factory, Tony used his contacts to bring nearly 50 workers from Sichuan for employment in Singapore. This was just the beginning and as demand for skilled workers increased, he founded Asia-Link Technology in 1994. Today with Tony at its helm, Asia-Link Technology is a sought after provider of human resource solutions in Singapore.

Integration: a two-way street

Tony candidly admits that due to its small size, job opportunities in Singapore are limited. Furthermore, the arrival of too many foreigners have become a point of contention with local Singaporeans, who resent their jobs being taken away by foreigners. Yet, the falling birth rate and the need for skilled blue-collar workers make the arrival of foreign workers inevitable. Since Singapore values diversity and thrives on attracting the best talents from all parts of the world, there is a need for enhancing inclusiveness and harmony in social and work life.

In his early days here, Tony would often get together with friends and old classmates from Sichuan to socialize. Gradually, as more immigrants started to join this eclectic group to celebrate traditional festivals such as Chinese New Year and Mid-Autumn Festival, Tony saw the need to create a platform where they could voice their opinions, exchange ideas and provide networking opportunities while fostering Singaporean culture and work ethics. In 1998, the Tian Fu Tong Xiang came about as a club for Sichuan natives. It became a venue where members, who were all immigrants, could encourage, help and support each other.

Today the Tian Fu Association (Singapore) — as the club is now called — has expanded to include immigrants from all over China. Registered in the year 2000, it has the noble aim of "helping new immigrants integrate into Singapore's multiracial society, build a cultural, scientific, technological and economical bridge between Singapore and China and provide information to members; to enrich the spare time lives of members and their families through various activities."

Keeping in mind Singapore's multicultural milieu, the Tian Fu Association organizes visits to places of worship such as mosques and Hindu temples, grassroots organizations, and arranges talks and seminars on Singapore's history and culture so that its members can understand Singapore society better. To inspire and motivate, members share stories about how they built their careers in Singapore and the Singaporean traditions and principles they've observed and abide by. A bi-monthly magazine published by the association helps new Chinese immigrants connect on a common platform and create a social and business network making it easier for them to settle in. Many members have made Singapore their home and Tony is justifiably proud of "turning a foreign land into a hometown and a hometown into a home, where roots are planted and the leaves are spread."

In 2011, the Singapore Federation of Chinese Clan Associations (SFCCA), of which Tony has been a long-time council member, honoured the Tian Fu Association for its role in promoting Chinese culture and social harmony. Taking a leaf out of Tony's book, many Chinese immigrants, hoping to integrate better into mainstream Singapore society, have taken up leadership positions at SFCCA.

Tony is also a member of the National Integration Council and hopes that he will be able to spread awareness about the contributions of new immigrants to society. In the past, he has been a member of REACH (Policy Study Workgroup on Population and Integration) and a feedback member of the Taxpayer Feedback Panel. A self-confessed optimist, Tony is happiest when throwing himself wholeheartedly into any cause that he espouses.

Tony believes that integration is not a one-way street and that Singaporeans should also play their part by trying to learn about the culture and habits of new immigrants, wherever they come from. This will broaden their understanding and help them respect each other better. That's why he is appreciative of the efforts of the Singapore government to send many youngsters to study in China, which, he opines, has been a step in the right direction.

Integrating naturally and wholeheartedly

In 1994, within a few years of moving here, Tony and his family took up Singapore citizenship. "It was the right choice," he says.

Adapting to their new life here was no walk in the park. In China, his wife had worked for the influential Sichuan Women's Federation and was given the opportunity to further her studies in Canada and Hong Kong, which she had to forego. After moving to Singapore, she supported Tony by taking on work as a cosmetic salesperson. His then eight-year-old son studied twice as hard as he was not proficient in English. The long hours and dedication that they all put in, paid dividends. His wife moved up rapidly in her job and his son, by sheer merit and hard work, went on to study at premier educational institutions in Singapore and abroad. While studying Political Science at the University of Michigan, he even garnered an internship at the Canadian Parliament. The family is well amalgamated in the Singapore way of life and is grateful that they can still follow the traditions and culture of their home country.

"Singapore is an extraordinary country that has successfully overcome the constraints of a tiny nation to win international respect. The government is transparent, people-friendly and humane." His only wish for Singapore is to continue to let people of all ethnic groups live and work in peace as naturalized citizens, contributing to the prosperity and stability of Singapore.

Singapore is now his motherland, and without hesitation Tony considers himself to be Singaporean.

A FAMILY ROOTED BY A SENSE OF BELONGING AND OWNERSHIP

"This is a country where regardless of your standing in life you get equal treatment."

Veena Prakash

Originally from the state of Jharkhand, India, work first brought Prakash Kejriwal to Singapore in 1995. His wife Veena followed him two years later. Their son Laavanya and daughter Esha were both born here and know no other home.

"I fell in love with this clean, green city and its people," says Veena, looking back at her years as a young bride who explored the island by public transport and enjoyed the freedom of being on her own, all the while feeling safe.

She easily adapted to her new life in Singapore and, on the advice of a Chinese friend, pursued a course to become an insurance agent.

Having their heart in the right place

It was when the children started school that Veena met more Singaporeans. Her daughter, whose closest friends are Chinese, would often bring them over. Veena and her husband also made it a point to invite their local friends home on special occasions and cook Indian food for them.

The family's close interaction with Singaporeans has made them appreciative of the local culture and way of life, and they became citizens in 2018. Veena sees similarities in familial values such as taking care of aged parents and honouring and respecting them, values she and her husband grew up with. Another thing that she has observed about Singaporeans is their ability to live together yet respect one another's independence and privacy.

Meeting Prime Minister Lee Hsien Loong casually at a concert a few years ago is something Veena will never forget. Her admiration for him increased manifold when she saw how friendly, relaxed and open he was mingling with ordinary citizens like her. "In Singapore, the leaders make an effort to wear appropriate clothes when they attend events of different races.

When I was complaining of the heat and discomfort of wearing a saree at an event, the PM wore Indian pants, kurta and a shawl. It was heartwarming and strangely humbling," elaborates Veena.

Veena modestly calls herself a "jack of all trades and master of none". Along with a partner, she runs Vmall Entertainment, an events management company. Their first sold-out exhibition was held at the Chinese Swimming Club in 2010, where Indian, Chinese and Caucasian entrepreneurs showcased their products, ranging from household items to clothes, jewellery and furniture. Beauty treatments and tailoring services were offered. Veena ensured that goods were sold at a reasonable price which added to the popularity of the bazaars. Since then, they have held several exhibitions and bazaars annually, which are overwhelmingly popular for the sheer variety of goods that they manage to source year after year.

She also organizes cultural events under the Vmall banner. Veena is pleased that through their Holi and Dandiya events, they have the opportunity to showcase Indian festivals to people from other communities. Dandiya evenings featuring Bollywood style music, Bollywood dancing and traditional dancing have gained popularity in recent times. "Interacting and participating in each other's social celebrations helps to foster mutual understanding, respect and social cohesion," she says. She recalls a Chinese freelance photographer who would keep track of their events so that he could take colourful and happy photographs of ordinary Singaporeans letting their hair down and enjoying the festivities.

Since 2017, her company has introduced Singaporeans to talented and renowned Indian artists, such as the eminent poet, filmmaker and writer Gulzar; tabla maestro Ustad Zakir Hussain; and popular Pakistani actor Fawad Khan.

More recently, in 2020, Vmall Entertainment brought together five world-class musicians for a delightful evening of fusion music blending jazz and Indian classical forms. Music transcends language and continents, and in the audience were Chinese, Indians, Malays and Caucasians. There were also concertgoers who specially flew in from Indonesia, Malaysia and New Zealand. Veena feels immensely gratified at the warm response and is already planning her next event where the audience can once again connect and come together as Singaporeans.

For Veena, success means working hard and keeping the artists and audiences happy and asking for more. The values of accountability, teamwork and effective communication rank high in her book. These are the very qualities that characterize the way the Singapore government functions and she finds Singapore society open, adaptable and talent-focused. Veena tries to incorporate these qualities in everything that she pursues.

Together we can

Her family remains her priority. Son Laavanya has completed his National Service and is now studying at a university overseas. He is confident that he did the right thing by choosing to serve the nation and understands the ethos of what it means to be a soldier. "If conscription was not mandatory, very few people would volunteer," he says. "Singaporeans should be combat ready in case the need arises. National Service bolsters the armed forces and keeps the nation safe." During the course of his training, he got to experience incidents that made him more aware of the social issues that many Singaporeans face daily, issues which he had never been exposed to.

Laavanya has played cricket since he was eight years old and even captained the Raffles Institution C & B Division Cricket team. But his biggest achievement was being part of the Singapore Under-16 National team. Having travelled extensively with his family, the young lad has come to appreciate the economic prosperity, political stability and well-thought-out national policies of Singapore. "Singapore has a certain standing in the world today in the way it conducts itself on the international stage. Even though the issues we face are constantly evolving and may pose challenges, Singapore can deal with them rationally and maturely." He says the label "Uniquely Singaporean" fits him well as he loves to 'chope' seats and breaks into Singlish when excited.

Esha, her daughter, is more laid back and considers herself a good mix of Singapore and India. Even though she has been brought up in a very Indian environment, the local culture and language have become an inherent part of her nature. "I think my biggest Singaporean trait is that I am *kiasu*," referring to the vernacular Chinese phrase for fear of losing out. She feels her family is not very different from the average Singaporean family as they are filial, visit relatives and celebrate birthdays and special occasions together, much like the locals. "My race may be Indian but my heart is Singaporean and I would not fit in anywhere else," says the teenager. She is confident that she can bridge the gap of being a first-generation Indian in Singapore and contribute to the nation as she has been brought up with Singaporean values. Esha is glad that her father decided to stay here.

Her father Prakash has a demanding job and travels extensively for work. He goes to Uzbekistan very often and is probably the most well-known Singaporean there. The family jokes that it was because of his frequent travels to the Central Asian country that Uzbekistan decided to waive off visa requirements for all Singaporeans!

Prakash is stress free when he travels because he is confident that when he is away, his family is safe. Even in the face of the Covid-19 outbreak and before that during the SARS crisis, he never doubted Singapore's ability to pull through. "Singapore is well equipped with the best medical resources. The government proactively quells rumours and shares information, and this gives me confidence that we are in safe hands."

The Kejriwal family, though Hindu, follows the religion of humanity. They are as comfortable celebrating Deepavali as they are the Lantern Festival. When their children were younger, they would walk the brightly lit streets of Chinatown during Chinese New Year, munching on freshly roasted peanuts and being a part of the festivities. A strict vegetarian, Veena doesn't cook or bring non-vegetarian food home, but her children and husband have given in to the temptation of Singapore's culinary delights and relish all kinds of local fare.

To this day, when she sees planes flying past her window in preparation for the National Day parade, a feeling of pride overwhelms Veena. She proudly sings the national anthem with her hand on her heart, for this is home!

The Kejriwals have embraced Singapore because Singapore has embraced them with open arms.

DANCING
IN STEP
WITH TIME

"I did not want to limit
Apsaras Arts to being just
an Indian dance company.
I had hoped it would be
a Singaporean company.
Today it has become
much more. We are now
Southeast Asian. We have
taken Indian dance to
another paradigm."

**Aravinth
Kumarasamy**

It is not often that one comes across an individual who excels in presenting various art forms to the world in a traditional manner, yet manages to push boundaries and create performances that appeal to audiences across cultures and languages.

Aravinth Kumarasamy is one such versatile artist who does not limit himself to a signature style. Instead, the artist in him evolves continuously. As the Artistic Director of Apsaras Arts, Aravinth has presented highly acclaimed stage shows where he has been involved in almost every aspect of production. Beating the trend of blending elements of Western dance forms with Indian classical dance, he has looked eastwards, creating new choreography, music and content, and is a name to reckon with in the performing arts scene in Southeast Asia. His productions have redefined the boundaries of Bharatanatyam ensemble work.

An unconventional career opportunity

Aravinth spent his formative years in Sri Lanka immersed in the Indian classical arts. A Sri Lankan Tamil by birth, he learnt the veena (a stringed musical instrument), Carnatic music and Bharatanatyam from a young age. Since these were considered nothing more than hobbies, he also trained professionally as a computer specialist.

Aravinth moved to Singapore in the late 80s and quickly became active in the local arts scene. While juggling a day job in the IT industry, the multi-talented artist pursued his interests as a faculty member at the Temple of Fine Arts and played the veena for Bhaskar's Arts Academy. He also composed music for various events and taught freelance at the Kallang Community Centre. Recognizing early on the need for an Indian orchestra, Aravinth established the immensely popular Kolam-Ayer Indian Youth Ensemble, funded by the People's Association (PA). It is from here that many of the blossoming young Indian talents of today had their beginnings.

Even while working in London where he was posted for some years, Aravinth would make the journey back to Singapore to attend arts events. On one such occasion, Senior Minister Tharman Shanmugaratnam and Ambassador Tommy Koh both asked him when he would be returning for good. That set him thinking more seriously. "Apart from Singapore, where else in the world is a minority community given equal status, appreciation and respect? It was time to come back," he recalls.

And so, when Mrs Neila Sathyalingam, the founder of Apsaras Arts, invited him to take up the position of Artistic Director in 2005, Aravinth did not think twice. In a leap of faith, Aravinth, who was already high up in the corporate ladder, quit his job and joined the dance company. It was a life-changing decision, and a most satisfying one.

A company with a heart and soul

Today Aravinth runs Apsaras Arts like a professional repertory company. Leveraging his corporate experience, he has applied industry best practices to turn it into something more than a teaching institute. Apsaras Arts started its own production with tickets being sold through the box-office. All aspects of what needed to be done to improve the quality of its offerings were looked into and improvements made.

Very early on in his career, in 1999, Aravinth was honoured with the Young Artist Award by the National Arts Council for his role in flying the Singapore flag overseas through creating, choreographing and presenting Indian dance programmes at international festivals. "I was the only permanent resident to have been chosen for this honour," says Aravinth, who took up Singapore citizenship the very next year, 2000, with justifiable pride.

Aravinth has an enormous and highly distinctive body of work and has pioneered a new benchmark of excellence through his innovative productions. As a prominent member of the Indian arts community, he has always looked beyond his brand and kept his Singaporean identity at the forefront. He has collaborated with Malay and Chinese organizations. The *Story of Radin Mas* was a local story based on Malay poetry. *Alapadma* drew its inspiration from the lotus flower and explored its representation in mythology, iconography and philosophy of the ancient civilizations of India, Iran, Egypt and Southeast Asia. It was staged at the Esplanade in 2015.

He has composed original musical scores for the PA on numerous occasions. For the Inaugural Indian Heritage Centre CulturalFest in 2015, he presented a dance concert *Natya Darpana* portraying the various Indian festivals celebrated in Singapore. It featured Singapore's leading Bharatanatyam dancers and choreographers. The music concert *Dina Raga Maalika* featured established and upcoming musicians performing vocal and instrumental Indian classical music.

Apsaras Arts have also collaborated with dance troops from other Southeast Asian countries, enabling Aravinth to reinvent the traditional while staying within conventional boundaries. Some examples of this are collaborations with the Javanese Dance Theatre, Jokjakarta, the National Balinese Dance Ensemble and the National Dance Company of Cambodia.

In 2019, Aravinth presented *Natya Shastra*, an ancient treatise on Indian dance traditions, at the 70th anniversary celebrations of the Singapore Indian Fine Arts Society (SIFAS) to showcase 100 years of Indian classical dance in Singapore.

The roots of another dance production *Agathi,* meaning refugee, which was first performed in 2018, lie in his own childhood experience of having to leave his home country Sri Lanka due to a civil war in which his family lost their home and had to flee to India. It deals with the plight of displaced refugees and has resonated with the immigrant community.

He regularly takes his productions to appreciative audiences in Malaysia, Indonesia, Sri Lanka, Australia and Europe, and has partnered with Esplanade Theatres by the Bay in Singapore to showcase his work.

His production of *Anjaneyam: Hanuman's Ramayana* was performed in November 2017 to sold-out shows at the Esplanade. This cross-cultural production was the result of a creative collaboration between the Era Dance Theatre (Singapore), Kalakshetra Repertory Theatre (India) and Bimo Dance Theatre (Indonesia), and leveraged the shared heritage of the ancient epic *Ramayana* in Southeast Asia.

Every project inspires Aravinth to reach for the next level. So when the Covid-19 crisis hit and many gigs were cancelled, Aravinth tailored his performances to enable audiences to watch them online. His first creation, a dance piece titled *Gratitude,* was a tribute to healthcare workers and frontline fighters of the pandemic for their service and for keeping humanity safe during this difficult time. It was released on social media to an appreciative audience.

Apsaras Arts was quick to adopt digital technology to showcase legendary artists speaking on a variety of topics. This gave them a larger audience as enthusiasts from all over the world could watch these events live. He concedes that the situation is artistically challenging, yet he is full of plans for the future.

Aravinth is acutely aware that he has a heritage to uphold and has tried to keep his art relevant to the younger generation. Especially so as in 2020, Apsaras Arts was one of the inaugural recipients of the Stewards of Intangible Cultural Heritage Award presented by the National Heritage Board. The award reinforced in him the need to nurture the living tradition of Indian dance and hand it over to the next generation of Singaporeans.

He believes that as an organization, Apsaras Arts is serving two kinds of people. "First are the audiences who are thirsty for something more. They are thoughtful, appreciative, and open to experiments. Then there are both established and upcoming artists who gain exposure, widen their horizon and get diverse opportunities by being associated with the group," he elaborates.

Another of Aravinth's brainchild is Dance India Asia Pacific, a dance education programme which he started in 2011. For the last nine years, he has curated talks, performances, master classes and book launches which take place across multiple venues in Singapore. There is something for everyone — the student, practitioner, teacher, connoisseur, and anyone interested in culture. Before the pandemic, delegates would fly in from around the world to perform or just to enjoy the performances and workshops. Now, the programme is a blend of physical and online sessions.

Aravinth has several national and international awards to his name, but it is the Kala Ratna Award, given to him by Singapore Indian Fine Arts Association, that particularly means a lot to him as it came from the community and fraternity.

Aravinth sits on the Advisory Board of the National Arts Council and the Talent Advisory Board of the People's Association advising on the national agenda for the arts. He feels that the arts can become a medium for locals and new immigrants to come together. Through various art forms they can learn to appreciate the diverse cultural heritage of Singapore and understand the cultural nuances of its multiracial society.

"Singapore is constantly evolving. New citizens should keep their antennas up, grow with it and stay relevant," he says. "That's what we did at Apsaras Arts as well, to turn it into a vibrant performing arts company which is in step with the times."

SERVICE, LEADERSHIP AND GIVING BACK TO THE COMMUNITY

"Success doesn't mean money. Little episodes of motivation, of giving back and making a difference in society make me feel I am doing something worthwhile and keep me going."

Sameen Khan, PBM

She came to Singapore as a young bride in 2007 and took to the city-state as a duck takes to water. By her admission a very adaptable person, Sameen Khan quickly set about building her home here. It was not too difficult, she recalls. Her husband had lived in Singapore for much longer and already had a wide social circle. Irrespective of race and religion, his friends became hers too. From welcoming her at the airport, to showing her around and explaining how to travel by MRT, they took her under their wing.

A Pakistani by birth, Sameen had been working in a pharmaceutical company before marriage. In Singapore, she volunteered with several organizations until grassroots work drew her attention. Once she signed up, she was pulled headlong into it and has not looked back since. Grassroots work gave her a direction and her extensive volunteer experience came in handy. She plays a very active part in the local community and is grateful for the opportunity to serve it. "I take things as they come," explains Sameen, "and that helped me settle down quickly in Singapore."

Getting inspired by causes that make a difference
Sameen has been a dedicated grassroots leader for the last decade or so, having held several official positions over the years. Currently, she chairs the River Valley Neighbourhood Committee (NC), and is a member of the Henderson-Dawson Citizens' Consultative Committee and the Resident's Network Council.

Sameen enjoys her work because she strongly believes in what she does, which is to make a difference in people's lives. She discloses that she has a three-pronged policy.

The first is to engage with as many people as she can. She encourages them to attend not just the many events the

NC organizes but join any kind of activities to promote neighbourliness, harmony and cohesiveness among residents. She is especially keen to draw the expatriate community into society and bring the locals out to meet the foreigners. The River Valley area, with its many private residential estates, is home to a unique mix of people. River Valley NC members make constant efforts to engage with the residents in their condominiums and she is proud that their outreach is substantial. She is well-connected to them and is there for anyone who needs help.

For special occasions, the NC counts on the strong relationships it has built with neighbourhood schools and businesses. Such collaboration has not only given them access to venues to hold their events, among other benefits, but has helped to strengthen community ties between the citizenry and businesses, explains Sameen.

Secondly, she partners with government agencies and works closely with organizations like the Singapore Police Force, NParks and National Environment Agency to address resident feedback. Issues that may seem ordinary, but which can become major irritants if ignored, are diffused quickly. For example, even before motorized Personal Mobility Devices were banned, her NC worked with the Land Transport Authority to implement the Active Mobility Act to enable a safer sharing of public paths among users. The NC is also an active participant in the Citizens on Patrol scheme. Here, volunteers patrol the neighbourhood, give out advisories on crime prevention, speak to residents, and report to the police on issues regarding safety and security that residents raise. Regular recce of the neighbourhood has helped foster good citizenship among residents.

Thirdly, Sameen is always on the lookout for ways that may help her serve the residents better. A Computer Science graduate with an MBA degree, she has taken active steps to change the way her NC connects with people. During the Covid-19 crisis, for instance, they shared the challenges facing the nation, listened to residents' feedback and reassured them that they would be looked after.

If there is a problem, Sameen makes it a point to not just listen but to get to the root of it and ensure it is resolved. She is aware of the issues and gaps that need to be filled and is ever ready to help. "Even when I am out for a casual walk I keep my eyes and ears open to anything in the neighbourhood that may need my attention," reveals Sameen.

Social media is used to spread awareness about new laws and policies and under Sameen's leadership, the Facebook page of River Valley NC has become more active. The NC also distributes flyers directly to the residents' letter boxes informing them of upcoming events and government advisories. "We are the link between people to people, people to Government and Government to people." She is lucky, she says, that she has a bunch of good people serving with her, all united in their commitment to bring the residents together.

"I believe in service leadership, working together, giving guidance, being flexible and adaptable, while empowering and engaging people," articulates Sameen. Her desire to serve comes from within, and in 2018 she was awarded the Pingat Bakti Masyarakat (PBM) for her efforts.

Balancing time between family, work and the community
The mother of two has her days planned out in a strict routine that helps her glide through them smoothly. Her son and daughter study in neighbourhood schools. Singapore is a good place to bring up kids, she says. They are growing up learning

to live in harmony and understanding multiculturalism, all the while having a sense of security and belonging.

For a few years, Sameen ran her own IT company. Looking back, she remembers it was one of only two companies in Singapore dealing with Augmented Reality and other projects and handling a large number of clients. She currently works for a digital start-up.

The lifelong learner, who is an avid photographer in her leisure time, enjoys being an agent of change and getting things done. She is also a believer in gaining new skills and has taken courses in teaching and digital marketing to improve herself.

The meritocratic system that Singapore is known for has made it possible for Sameen, a naturalized citizen, to be leading an NC. She took every opportunity that came her way. "When I joined the NC I had a lot of time on my hands. The more I did, the more I wanted to do, and I was given the opportunity to do it," she declares passionately. Sameen has been the Chairperson for over five years. Before that, she served as the Assistant Secretary and Secretary.

Her grassroots work has helped her connect with Singapore and Singaporeans. She counts racial harmony as one of Singapore's strengths since it has made Singaporeans open-minded and respectful of each other's cultures and traditions.

Shortly after taking up Singapore citizenship in 2012, she was invited to sing the National Anthem at a National Day dinner. "There were a lot of emotions running through my mind," she confesses. "There was a feeling of belonging and of being welcomed in the fold combined with respect and desire to give back. It was my first opportunity to represent Singapore and it was important for me to put my best foot forward."

"I have achieved more than I thought I was capable of and I know I can still do better." Sameen knows that with every honour comes a responsibility. It's not the PBM that she received in 2018 but the expectations that come with it that she tries to live up to. For her, it is not mere reciprocity but a genuine heartfelt desire to give back to her country. "As new citizens, we must continue to respect our roots but be loyal to Singapore," says Sameen.

GIVING TILL IT HURTS

"Seeing the plight of those who are suffering makes me grateful for what I have. Being able to help in my small way is what gives me a lot of pleasure."

Rajan Jain

When news of Mr Rajan Jain donating $1 million to start a charitable trust broke in early 2021, most people in Singapore were taken by surprise. He was no staggeringly wealthy philanthropist, but just an ordinary citizen, and a naturalized one at that, who was willing to pledge half his retirement savings to a worthy cause.

Rajan had come to Singapore in 2002 to set up the regional office of a German company. Having travelled extensively the world over, he was attracted to the work culture, rule of law and strong governance that is synonymous with Singapore. Within a few months, he moved his family here, taking up Singapore citizenship in 2005.

Defining moments

Rajan was born in the United States to Indian parents. His father made it a point to tell his five children stories from the Hindu scriptures to reinforce universal values such as respect for women, teachers, elders, the poor, as well as *sewa* or service to others. These early and informal moral lessons became the pillars of Rajan's value system and shaped his personality.

Rajan moved back to India in his teens. Wanting to learn more about his roots, he hitchhiked around the country and was affected by the misery he saw around him. His parents had also exposed him to the plight of the needy and would take the family to orphanages on special occasions to distribute food to the children. With four older siblings, Rajan was used to sharing his things, and as the youngest child it was quite normal for him to wear hand-me-downs and use old textbooks, he recalls. His upbringing thus played a big part in moulding Rajan's giving personality.

A turning point came when the young Rajan got an opportunity to meet Mother Teresa, the Nobel laureate who had given up a life of comfort to serve the sick and dying on the streets of Kolkata. Mother Teresa told him to "give till it hurts".

"I did not have it in me to be as caring or fearless as Mother Teresa, but she inspired me to do what I was capable of," says Rajan. The first thing he did was to keep aside 10 per cent of his salary for the needy, a habit he continues to this day.

Over 30 years ago, along with a friend, Rajan set up Asra, a charitable trust in Mumbai, India, with the noble aim of helping people across communities and religions. Rajan estimates that Asra, which means 'support' in Urdu, has over the years put over 2,000 children through school and helped pay the medical and rehabilitation fees for countless needy people.

"We receive 20 to 25 letters each day and sift through them very carefully to find the right people to help," says Rajan of Asra today. He admits that in the early years, people took advantage of his naivety. He has also been deceived by fraudsters pretending to need help. He has learnt his lesson and no longer donates directly to the beneficiary but makes payments to the hospital or educational institution as required. These negative experiences, however, have neither disheartened him nor made him lose faith in humanity.

He is gratified when the beneficiaries who do well in life offer to pay back the money spent on them. But he tells them to pay it forward instead. Many of them do so by supporting Asra through donations or by mentoring younger beneficiaries, or just helping society in any way they can. Asra remains a lean organization where 99 per cent of the funds are earmarked for charity. Only 1 per cent goes towards running the organization.

Helping others in need
Rajan is lucky to have married a lady who has backed him wholeheartedly in his endeavours and supported him every

step of the way. Be it his decision to help the needy or move to Singapore, she has taken it all in her stride, stepping up to help with Asra when required or helping the family adapt to their new life in Singapore.

She and Rajan are volunteers with the Singapore Prison Services' Befriending Programme. As befrienders, they give moral support and guide inmates over a period of 16 months, to help them integrate back into society. It is not easy to befriend or mentor an offender, admits Rajan, especially because emotions are involved. Their reward however is in seeing the offender being accepted back by their families and into mainstream society.

When approached, Rajan doesn't hesistate to provide financial help to those in need. He has helped patients at the Changi General Hospital with their medical bills. At the height of the Covid-19 crisis when many foreign workers fell ill with the virus, he gifted 300 phone cards to enable them to talk to their loved ones in their home countries. "Every person is my own," he says humbly, "all that is required is an attitude for charity."

It is this attitude that made Rajan think of donating a large chunk of his retirement money into a trust. "As soon as I received the money, I put it aside so that I would not be tempted to use it for myself. He admits that the thought of pumping these funds into Asra did cross his mind, but he decided against it, preferring to share it with his adoptive country that he so admires and that has given him and his family a forever home they can be proud of.

He began to lay the groundwork to set up a charitable trust in Singapore. The Committee of Charities screened him thoroughly to check the genuineness of his intentions. His persistence paid off and he received the requisite approval to set up Sunshine Trust in 2020.

"When you give money, you have to give with the right intention," says Rajan. "A charity has to keep its nose to the ground and be aware of the social situation. Just as in Asra, I wanted a name that did not have any strings attached to it but drew attention to my desire to bring sunshine in the lives of those facing difficulties," he explains.

Through the Sunshine Trust, he aims to help underprivileged Singaporeans with their medical fees, education, or any other pressing needs. His wife and two adult children, a son and a daughter, are trustees of the fund. Should his family not be interested in running the trust, the Commission of Charities will continue to run it.

Rajan is an avid reader. His interests include books on Singapore's history, including the memoirs of former Prime Minister Lee Kuan Yew, a man whom Rajan admires deeply.

He enjoys his retirement taking long walks in parks and nature reserves, spending time with his grandchildren, and helping his daughter set up her business. His son has completed his National Service and higher education in Singapore, and is looking forward to joining the workforce soon. Rajan is thankful that both his children grew up in Singapore, where the right social values and discipline were instilled in them.

Content to live out his retirement years with minimum wants, Rajan sees the Sunshine Trust as his last chance to do something beneficial for society. He is a man who walks the talk.

CREATING A KINDER SOCIETY

"What brought Singapore here is its determination to be one nation and one people, but now there is a need to open our minds to new ideas in education, economics, politics and the social sphere. Thankfully, younger Singaporeans are moving in the right direction."

Cesar Balota

He claims his first impression upon landing in Singapore in 1979 was that of shock. Nothing had prepared Cesar Balota for the "efficiency, orderliness and cleanliness" of the Little Red Dot. Forty-one years later, he confesses he also found Singapore too "sterile, boring and organized" for his happy-go-lucky spirit.

But the Filipino, who had been transferred here by his employer, soon felt at ease as local friends invited him to their homes, checked on him after office hours and helped him navigate his new surroundings. After all these years, he still keeps in touch with them, meeting up at weddings, Christmas and Chinese New Year.

Work kept him busy, and he fit right in with the meritocratic work culture that Singapore espouses, soon learning to appreciate how everything in Singapore was super organized, safe and worked with clockwork precision.

Home is where the heart is

Within a year, Cesar met and began dating a Singaporean Chinese girl. They married soon after and have a son and daughter. Having a young family prompted him to take up permanent residency here. Being married to a local girl, he says, was a sign that he was comfortable with the country and its people. Her friends became his and vice versa.

He has conquered his unfamiliarity with Singaporean food, has many favourites, and now prefers the spicy curry that comes with his roti prata over the sugar that he initially ate with this crispy South Indian flat bread. He has also picked up the local accent switching easily with his Filipino accent. And when he returns after travelling overseas, he always feels a sense of homecoming.

While his wife has learnt to cook Filipino dishes, home cooked meals are now a mix of local, Filipino and Western fare. He looks slightly bemused as he notes that these days he goes to Filipino restaurants only when his local friends ask for Filipino food. Every Christmas, he decorates his home with a *parol*, a colourful ornamental star-shaped lantern that is part of the Christmas tradition in the Philippines.

Cesar's children are immersed in the Singaporean culture. They studied in local schools and took Mandarin as their second language. His son went through the rigours of National Service and, like his father, married a Singaporean Chinese. Cesar has two grandchildren who are "true blue Singaporeans". In 1989, Cesar became a citizen of Singapore.

Filipinos are, by and large, flexible and easy going, and Cesar is no exception. He is not one to stress over trifles, although initially it bothered him to see Singaporeans take everything seriously, even prioritizing work over leisure. He hardly finds anyone singing, he says, except on National Day when Singaporeans burst into song! When his children were young and he had to take them to events and birthday parties, he would break the ice by singing fun songs and encourage the other children to join in.

Kindness: A gift everyone can afford to give

His early years in Singapore were taken up by his job and family commitments. Volunteering was limited to church activities, counselling and mentoring the youth at his church.

In 2011, the company that Cesar worked for was acquired and Cesar was released. With his children grown up, he suddenly found himself with time on his hands. His thoughts shifted to volunteering and he felt the call to help the less fortunate. Through his church, he started participating in outreach programmes and visited neighbouring countries on aid missions. He was part of one of the earliest church teams that travelled to northeast Japan to help victims of the tsunami that struck the region in 2011. He continued to visit Japan every year to work with the elderly but that stopped in 2020 when the Covid-19 pandemic raged globally. Today, he is part of a committee that does outreach work with street children and serves on the governing board of another which helps to train pastors of churches in the region. In doing these, he sees himself as a proud ambassador of Singapore.

During this time, Mr William Wan of Singapore Kindness Movement (SKM) convinced him to join the organization. Cesar agreed and as Associate General Secretary, he was responsible for SKM's strategic direction, branding and public engagement.With his marketing background, Cesar came up with a social media programme and other campaigns which he felt would resonate with Singaporeans and engage them. He targeted younger audiences as he wanted them to be drawn into becoming the instruments of change.

He had planned to be with the NGO for two years, but ended up being involved with them for eight years. "My initial aim was to build up the work scope and train a successor to take over from me. However, SKM expanded, and I continued as I was contributing meaningfully to it," says Cesar. He stepped down in 2019 as he felt he had given what he could, and it was time for someone else to take the programme forward.

In 2013, when the SKM mascot 'Singa the Lion' was resigned, Cesar received a lot of flak and was branded as a "foreigner who tampered with a national symbol and had the audacity to teach Singapore about graciousness". By then a citizen for 24 years, he took the criticism in stride, noting that kindness is a universal human value and had nothing to do with his foreign origins. He lets his work speak for him.

He strongly believes that SKM plays a critical role in making Singapore a kinder and more caring place and is glad that Singapore is moving ahead in the right direction. Younger Singaporeans, he feels, are now more than ever concerned and aware of social issues and consciously trying to make a positive impact in very real ways. When he comes across people who want to give back to society even when they have busy careers, he feels he has achieved what he had set out to do during his stint at SKM.

His wish is for Singapore to become even more inclusive and less polarized in opinion, not just towards foreigners, but across economic status and social standing, and accepting of alternate points of view.

Cesar recalls the time he came to Singapore: there were few immigrants and it was much easier to fit in and be accepted. While Singaporeans went out of their way to be nice, these new settlers on their part made conscious efforts to merge into the social milieu. However, as the numbers increased, the tendency to socialize more within their groups became an easy comfort in a new environment. He points out that it is important for immigrants to make a conscious effort to interact with Singaporeans, follow the local norms and culture, and respect the different ethnicities that make up Singapore. He, on his part, has not only assimilated in Singapore but also enriched it by bringing in the flavour of his own birth country here.

The naturalized Singaporean advocates a big dose of patience and a willingness to accept differences on both sides. "I have certainly learnt and benefitted from my life in Singapore. But I can also see the potential for Singapore as it takes in new immigrants not just for their functional skills but also for the new hues of social practices that they would add to the colours of the original settlers here. In learning from each other, we can make a truly kinder society. When this is recognized and celebrated, the integration circle would be complete," he concludes passionately.

EYEING BETTER MEDICAL CARE FOR ALL

"I think we are here in this world for a purpose. If we can't give back to society, we have wasted this life."

Dr Rupesh Agrawal

Access to healthcare and education irrespective of one's financial and social background: this is a cause Dr Rupesh Agrawal passionately believes in, and what he ideally wants to see in Singapore.

For Rupesh, a senior consultant ophthalmologist at Tan Tock Seng Hospital, it is his earnest hope that he can bring about a positive and sustained change to resolve this disparity. "Singapore has the resources to put an end to this inequality," he says.

Rupesh is also Adjunct Associate Professor at the Nanyang Technological University, and is affiliated with Duke NUS Medical School, Lee Kong Chian School of Medicine, Yong Loo Lin School of Medicine, University College London and Moorfields Eye Hospital, London.

In addition, he is a clinician scientist advancing cutting-edge research in eye care. What is more he is involved with many humanitarian projects aimed at providing the best possible eye care and education to the community in Singapore and overseas.

Adding more feathers to his cap

After completing his medical studies, Rupesh was lucky to be associated with some of the top research institutes and eye hospitals in India.

He moved to Singapore in 2009 and took up citizenship in 2011 having seen for himself that Singapore was an ideal place to raise his family. In addition, it offered him the opportunity to provide state-of-the-art treatment to his patients and help the less privileged. Becoming Singaporean gave Rupesh much needed stability to settle down and focus on medical research. In the same year, together with other recipients, he received the Healthcare Humanity Award by then President of Singapore,

S R Nathan; the award was given in recognition of his pro bono humanitarian projects in remote parts of the world.

He was also awarded an overseas research training fellowship by the Ministry of Health. Under this scheme, Rupesh spent the next few years as a researcher in the United Kingdom, at the Institute of Ophthalmology and University College London. He completed numerous research projects at the prestigious Moorfields Eye Hospital, London. If this was not enough, he simultaneously completed the Global Clinical Scholars Research Training (GCSRT) programme from Harvard Medical School.

His areas of research interest are systemic diseases involving the eye particularly related to bacterial and viral infections as well as ocular injuries.

Rupesh fully supports Singapore's policy of collaborating with overseas institutes. Collaboration is beneficial not just for scholars who are keen on research work but also benefits the country as participants gain knowledge from breakthrough research, create a strong overseas network and develop a broader outlook. Citing his example, he says that he had 120 articles published in medical journals just in the two years he was in London. He was able to pack in so much in a short time because of his strong desire to give back to the country that had allowed him to pursue his dreams. Today he has over 60 collaborations and numerous projects under his belt.

He has published several articles on the translational research he has conducted; these show how careful observation of the eye can give doctors a clue to the presence of diseases in other parts of the body such as human immunodeficiency virus (HIV), dengue, diabetes and high blood pressure, prompting patients to seek further advice and appropriate treatment. Even though more research is needed in this area, Rupesh has managed to draw attention to the eye as a diagnostic tool and helped put Singapore on the forefront of global research in the field of ophthalmology. For his research on tuberculosis of the eye, he was awarded first prize in the VSY Biotechnology Ophthalmology Star Awards in 2020.

During the Covid-19 pandemic, Rupesh conducted research to assess if the deadly virus could be transmitted through ocular fluids. He is rooting for better safety procedures and innovative strategies for ophthalmologists to employ during pandemics.

Serving causes and connecting communities

In his student days, Rupesh was often the first to enter the library and last to leave, choosing to spend all his leisure hours helping other students and becoming a mentor to many of them. His compassion for others is evident in the causes he has stood for.

In 2009, Rupesh had the opportunity to go to Bangladesh as part of a medical mission team and was deeply affected by the poor state of healthcare he witnessed. Resolving to do more, he has since led medical teams to Bangladesh, Nepal, Cambodia, India and many other countries. He has perfected the art of providing healthcare with limited resources, says Rupesh wryly.

He is a part of Project Aasha under which medical students of Lee Kong Chian School of Medicine go to Nepal to conduct free cataract surgery camps for the rural communities. Another initiative he is associated with is Project i2Eye, an overseas community involvement project led by students from the National University of Singapore. He accompanies the students to remote parts of India to improve the health of locals through health screenings and follow-up.

In 2016, Rupesh and his brother Dr Rohit Agrawal, an anaesthetist and fellow Singaporean, set up the non-profit Viraj

Healthcare Foundation. Together with volunteer doctors, they provide free healthcare to the community both locally and internationally.

He does all this work in his own time, on weekends or when he takes annual leave. As a family, they never take exotic vacations, preferring to give their time to people who need help. His teenage daughter travels with him and his wife, a dentist, is immensely supportive of his ventures. He confesses he couldn't have achieved half of what he has done without their support.

Rupesh values his early years in Singapore, when home was an HDB flat in Bishan. That is where he made long-term friends. These were the people who were his wife's support system when he was overseas. Even today they go back to their old estate to meet up with friends and it gives them immense joy to see the smiles of recognition on the faces of the aunties and uncles in the neighbourhood.

In 2018, he was presented with the prestigious President's Volunteerism & Philanthropy Award for his humanitarian projects.

Win-win partnerships
Rupesh wants to get youngsters involved in the community. He strongly believes that only by exposing Singaporeans to real-world settings can their eyes be opened to the harsh realities of life. He works closely with medical students and makes them a part of his charitable endeavours, motivating them to embrace issues pertinent to society. Seeing first-hand the difficulties patients in developing countries face helps them realize what it means to be a doctor and gives them a sense of direction.

He himself feels inspired by the fresh ideas that young people come up with since they are tech-savvy and have a different perspective on problems. He is happy if even a handful of students are inspired to lead initiatives of their own and become stakeholders, for only then will those projects continue to thrive, says Rupesh.

Giving back to society is something Rupesh learnt as a child, and he continues to live by his philosophy of social inclusion and serving causes that have been overlooked. He is grateful to his parents, teachers, mentors and colleagues for moulding him to be the person that he is today. He wants every Singaporean to contribute just one per cent of their time to Singapore, and look beyond themselves to cultivate a kinder, more caring and giving society.

Rupesh works hard to make a difference, is ready to venture on difficult paths and is passionate about his patients and community work. His biggest driving force is the inequality that he sees in the community and he dreams of a world where everyone is equal.

"There is still so much to be done. As a doctor, when I see a businessman, officer or a sweeper, should my attitude, body language and behaviour change?" he questions. He is disturbed to see patients in less developed countries sit before him with their hands folded in gratitude. "They have an equal right to the best medical care and as humans, we fail if we don't provide them with that."

Here is a man who derives much satisfaction and fulfilment by helping others and will not stop until he has achieved his goal.

ABOUT THE TEAM

Mr Prakash Kumar Hetamsaria, PBM

Mr Prakash Kumar Hetamsaria came to Singapore over a quarter of a century ago. Realizing that Singapore was where he would like to sink his roots and raise a family, he took up citizenship in 1999.

Over the years, Prakash, who is a qualified Chartered Accountant, a member of the Institute of Singapore Chartered Accountants and the CFO of an international trading company, has been involved in various grassroots organizations and immigrant associations. His experience as a naturalized citizen and grassroots leader has made him conscious of the need to give back to the community. He has helmed several projects and been a part of various committees, all with the aim to serve the community and foster meaningful integration between the locals and newcomers in Singapore. In 2021 he was awarded the PBM for his meritorious service to Singapore

In 2015, he published *Integration – Perspective of Naturalized Citizen*, describing his journey to becoming a Singaporean.

Prakash considers the principle of humanity to be above race and religion. A humble person, he does not mind going the extra mile to connect with the local community. With the objective of working towards creating an inclusive society, through social integration and community engagement, he, together with his wife Bhawana, have started a non-profit organization called ITSCommunityCare. Through it, they hope to help underprivileged members of the community and espouse social causes like the environment and climate change.

Mrs Vandana Aggarwal

An educator, archivist and a published author, Mrs Vandana Aggarwal wears many hats. After nearly 15 years of experience as a teacher, she decided to switch roles and go into freelance journalism.

She mostly writes on topics of cultural and historical interest. She has researched and shown a light on some hitherto unknown facets of Singapore history. One such effort culminated in her book, *Voice of Indian Women: The Kamala Club Singapore*. The book provided for the first time a chronological record of the pioneer Indian women's club in Singapore and its immense contribution to society.

Vandana's work has been published both in Singapore and abroad. She is well-known for her series of articles on the Indian Singaporean business families of yore and stories showcasing various Indian communities who have made Singapore their home.

As a volunteer transcriber for the National Archives of Singapore, she has transcribed over 11,000 pages of the Straits Settlement Records, thus playing a part in saving these fragile historical records for posterity.

Mr Baldeo Prasad

Mr Baldeo Prasad has a keen interest in photography and has been a member of the Photographic Society of Singapore since 2003. He is inspired by the beauty of nature which encourages him to capture the sublime moments before they fade away. Improvements in digital technology in photography let him click as much as he wishes without any constraint. Today, he takes photos of landscapes and nature as well as portraits for friends.